Contents

Contents

941.06

SEMINAR STUDIES IN HISTORY

General Editor: Roger Lockyer

Restoration England: The Reign of Charles II

John Miller

Reader in History
Queen Mary College
University of London

THE LIBRARY

WYCLIFFE COLLEGE, STONEHOUSE

GLOUCESTERSHIRE

HF

Restoration England: the reign of Charles II
108593

WITHDRAWN

Non-Fiction   0582353963   941.06 MIL
Wycliffe College

LONGMAN

London and New York

LONGMAN GROUP LIMITED
Longman House, Burnt Mill, Harlow, Essex CM20 2JE, UK
and Associated Companies throughout the World.
Published in the United States of America
by Longman Inc., New York

© Longman Group Limited 1985
All rights reserved; no part of this publication
may be reproduced, stored in a retrieval system,
or transmitted in any form or by any means, electronic
mechanical, photocopying, recording, or otherwise,
without the prior written permission of the Publishers.

First published 1985
ISBN 0 582 35396 3

Set in 10/11pt Linotron Baskerville

Produced by Longman Group (F.E.) Limited
Printed in Hong Kong

British Library Cataloguing in Publication Data

Miller, John
  Restoration England: the reign of Charles II.
  (Seminar studies in history)
  1. Great Britain — Politics and governments —
  1660–1688
  I. Title   II. Series
  942.06'6   DA445

  ISBN 0–582–35396–3

Library of Congress Cataloging in Publication Data

Miller, John (John L.)
  Restoration England.

  (Seminar studies in history)
  Bibliography: p.
  Includes index.
  1. Great Britain — History — Charles II, 1660–1685.
  2. Great Britain — Politics and government — 1660–1688.
  I. Title   II. Series.
  DA445.M45 1985   942.06'6   84–17169
  ISBN 0–582–35396–3

Seminar Studies in History
Founding Editor: Patrick Richardson

Introduction

The Seminar Studies series was conceived by Patrick Richardson, whose experience of teaching history persuaded him of the need for something more substantial than a textbook chapter but less formidable than the specialised full-length academic work. He was also convinced that such studies, although limited in length, should provide an up-to-date and authoritative introduction to the topic under discussion as well as a selection of relevant documents and a comprehensive bibliography.

Patrick Richardson died in 1979, but by that time the Seminar Studies series was firmly established, and it continues to fulfil the role he intended for it. This book, like others in the series, is therefore a living tribute to a gifted and original teacher.

Note on the System of References:
A bold number in round brackets (**5**) in the text refers the reader to the corresponding entry in the Bibliography section at the end of the book. A bold number in square brackets, preceded by 'doc'. [**doc. 6**] refers the reader to the corresponding item in the section of Documents, which follows the main text.

ROGER LOCKYER
General Editor

Acknowledgements

We are grateful to Richard Salwey Esq for permission to reproduce document 14; to the Clerk of the Records of the House of Lords for permission to reproduce document 13; and to the Bodleian Library for permission to reproduce document 20.

Cover: Marble bust of Charles II inscribed by sculptor: 1684 Honnore Pelle. Weidenfeld and Nicolson Ltd.

Preface

Historians' views of the reign of Charles II have often been coloured by what came before and after it. The 1640s and 1650s had seen civil war and the abolition of monarchy, while after the Glorious Revolution, although the monarch retained most of his traditional powers, he found it increasingly difficult to exercise them. It might seem, therefore, that the events of 1640–60 fatally weakened the foundations of monarchy and that this weakness was finally exposed after 1689. Such a view led many historians to ignore the Restoration period and to see 1640–60 as the definitive period of change in Stuart England. They therefore looked back well before 1640 for the long-term causes of this change. Others have been fascinated by the political and religious radicals who emerged in the 1640s and largely disappear from the historian's view after 1660. For many twentieth-century writers, if seventeenth-century English history did not end in 1660, it ceased to be interesting (**72**).

The last twenty years have, however, seen a renewed interest in the later Stuart period. A vast amount of research and speculation has failed to demonstrate that the civil war was the product of long-term social and economic changes, or that any major change occurred in the structure of England's economy and society. Recent studies have stressed the importance of chance and of accidents of personality in bringing about civil war. It has been argued that Charles I made a generally accepted constitution unworkable because of the distrust he created and that the misconceptions which Charles and Pym had about one another's intentions drove them to extreme measures (**59, 105**). These developments in the study of early Stuart history have important implications for that of the Restoration period, which has come to seem more worthy of study in its own right now that it appears that all the great issues of seventeenth-century English history had not, after all, been settled by 1660.

The reign of Charles II has been less intensively studied than the 1640s and the patchy state of our present knowledge is reflected in the chapters which follow. The Church and land settlements apart, no satisfactory study of the Restoration settlement has been published, so the first part of the book is based mainly on primary sources. In the second part, some sections are based on a solid body of research, published and unpublished, while others are more impressionistic and so likely to need substantial modification in the light of future research. I shall suggest that the Restoration settlement created the basis for a potentially viable and lasting regime. Had Charles II not inherited his father's capacity for inspiring mistrust, had he not shown so little political common sense, his reign might have been remembered as one of peace and harmony. As it was, when his conduct and that of his brother provoked a crisis which reminded contemporaries of that of 1640–2, he not only survived but crushed his enemies and lived out his last years without having to call Parliament. The causes of the Revolution of 1688 must be sought in James II's reign, not Charles II's, and that reign (which I have discussed elsewhere (**88, 89**)) is outside the scope of this book.

Part One: The Restoration

1   The End of the Interregnum

It might seem odd that Charles II's return to England in 1660 was greeted with almost universal rejoicing. Had not his father's subjects fought against and executed him? Had Charles not spent years in exile, with little prospect of regaining the crown? To explain the Restoration one must first seek to understand the events of 1640–60. Had the Parliamentarians* been seeking to destroy the monarchy, its subsequent restoration would indeed seem extraordinary, but most had no such intention. The great majority of the ruling elite wished, in the 1640s, to preserve the 'ancient constitution', with its balance between the powers of the Crown and the rights of the subject and its stress on taxation by consent and the rule of law. They saw that constitution as under threat, in one of two ways.

First, Charles I failed to govern in what his subjects regarded as a fair and reasonable manner. He sought to rule without Parliament, the traditional embodiment of government by consent. He stretched his fiscal rights to the limit in a way which might just be within the letter of the law, but was contrary to its spirit. Along with fiscal rapacity and chicanery went an authoritarian style of government. The JPs* who directed local government had traditionally, and wisely, been allowed a measure of discretion, adapting national regulations to suit local circumstances. Charles demanded that JPs carried out their instructions to the letter and added insult to injury by involving them in his unpopular fiscal expedients. Finally, his regime was increasingly tainted with 'Popery'. Archbishop Laud's emphasis on ritual and ceremony led to accusations that he was leading the Church of England back to Catholicism. Even more sinister was the influence at court of Catholics such as the queen, Henrietta Maria, and the papal nuncio, George Con (**59**).

By 1640 it was widely believed that Charles, or those about him, wished to establish Catholicism and absolutism.* A Scots invasion forced him to call Parliament and to abandon some of the institutions and most of the fiscal devices abused in the 1630s, but his

*Asterisked words are explained in the Glossary.

1

concessions did not lead to a settlement because of repeated indications that Charles wished to use force to reverse them. Fear of having their throats cut by bloodthirsty Popish soldiers drove many moderates to support demands (largely formulated by John Pym) which ran counter to their conservative principles, notably that Parliament should share in the king's control of the armed forces and in his choice of advisers. Most of those who supported such demands did not wish to weaken the monarchy or to increase Parliament's power: their motive was simple self-preservation, as was shown by Parliament's defensive strategy in the early part of the Civil War.

If one possible threat to the 'ancient constitution' was the forcible establishment of absolutism, the other emerged after the Long Parliament met. Some MPs denounced Pym's attempts to restrict the king's powers as novel and illegal. When the king and Lords resisted measures which the Commons' leaders saw as vital, the latter appealed to a wider public outside Parliament. The dramatic events of 1640–1 and the collapse of press censorship encouraged popular political debate. Londoners, fearful of the Papists and the king's soldiers, took to the streets in their thousands, striking fear into the king and peers. Meanwhile, the collapse of the bishops' authority allowed people to discuss religion and to worship as they wished. Taken together, these developments alarmed many of the ruling elite. Established authority in Church, state and society seemed to be under attack. If fear of absolutism led many conservative gentlemen to side with Parliament, fear of anarchy drove many others to support the king. 'The alteration of government,' wrote the Earl of Northumberland, 'is apprehended on both sides' (**59**).

At first, the majority in Parliament hoped that, if they could avoid defeat, Charles would have to negotiate. When it became clear that he would not do so, they were forced to adopt a more aggressive approach. The Solemn League and Covenant of 1643 secured valuable military help from the Scots, but at the price of a commitment to abolish bishops and to introduce some form of Presbyterianism*. Meanwhile, the war imposed a great burden on the people. Taxes were far heavier than ever before, and both sides' local agents often acted arbitrarily when mobilising men and munitions. The armies requisitioned, plundered and disrupted normal economic activity. By 1646 much of the popular support which Parliament enjoyed in 1642 had evaporated and the demand grew to end war taxation, disband the armies and return to normal. That, however, required a settlement with the king, and Charles still refused to make meaningful concessions.

By late 1648, worried by popular discontent and the army's new-found interest in politics, Parliament found its resolve weakening, which led the army to demand that Parliament break off negotiations. It refused, so on 6 December 1648 Colonel Pride arrested those MPs most outspokenly in favour of continuing negotiations and turned others away. Many more refused to take their seats, in protest. The remaining minority, or 'Rump', set up a high court of justice which tried and condemned the king: he was executed on 30 January 1649. Some weeks later the monarchy was abolished, along with the House of Lords, almost all the peers having withdrawn. England was declared a 'commonwealth or free state' (**115**).

Pride's Purge and Charles's execution were the pivotal events of the 'English Revolution'. They removed all hope of a negotiated settlement based on the traditional constitution, which had been a real possibility until the purge, and ensured that the regimes of the 1650s would be dependent on the army. The Parliamentarians* of the 1640s had been divided, but the Long Parliament had been legally convened and represented a large part of the nation. After Pride's Purge any claim to continuity or constitutionality was only a tenuous fiction. The Rump might talk of the sovereignty of the people and pose as the people's representative, but was well aware of its lack of support. Pride's Purge and Charles's execution were carried through by a small, unrepresentative minority. Most Parliamentarians (not to mention Royalists) abhorred both. The driving force behind them was the army, self-consciously separate from (and, in its own eyes, morally superior to) civilian society. It dealt easily with the last vestiges of opposition within the British Isles, but its civilian allies were few and disunited. That army rule did not degenerate into military tyranny owed much to Cromwell. He resisted the call of some of his officers to impose a 'dictatorship of the godly' and sought instead to heal the divisions of the civil war, by establishing a measure of civilian support for his regime (**36**).

The traditional vehicle for such support was Parliament, but to secure an amenable Parliament was not easy. Historians have devoted more attention to the small, mainly urban popular movements of this period, and to the radical sects, than their numbers merited. In the villages and market towns where most people lived, the overriding impression is of a population unaffected by political and religious radicalism, its conservatism maintained by illiteracy, inertia and poor communications (**55, 58, 94, 126**). The radicals lacked the numbers and political weight to form a viable civilian base for the republic. Those who counted politically were the landed elite (nobility and gentry) and the leading citizens of the towns, who would dominate any electoral system, thanks to their power as landlords, employers and consumers and the respect in which they were held by those lower down the social scale. Only a tiny minority of this elite wholeheartedly supported the regimes of the 1650s. The Royalists were irreconcilable, so the obvious source of support was from among the Parliamentarians*, notably those moderates, usually known as Presbyterians*, who had been alienated by Pride's Purge and the king's execution.

Unfortunately for Cromwell, the Presbyterians' views differed markedly from his. First, he was committed to religious liberty. He preserved the outward structure of a national church, with a minister in each parish supported by tithes*, but allowed the clergy a wide latitude in matters of worship and doctrine. Those who wished to worship elsewhere could do so, except for Papists or 'prelatists'. The Presbyterians believed in a single, fairly uniform church to which all should belong. This they saw as essential if moral discipline and theological orthodoxy were to be maintained. Secondly, Cromwell wished to preserve the army (not least as the guarantor of religious liberty); the Presbyterians thought it expensive, tyrannical and unacceptably radical, and longed to be rid of it. Thirdly, Cromwell (and the army) were committed to the republic. The Presbyterians believed in monarchy, preferably a Stuart monarchy. Such fundamental differences made long-term co-operation unlikely, unless Cromwell abandoned the army and ruled as the Presbyterians wanted. Many Presbyterians served in local government and sought election to Cromwell's Parliaments, but often did so merely in order to change or undermine his regime from within. Cromwell could work with his Parliaments only by circumscribing their powers and imposing political conditions on their members. When such restrictions were removed, they degenerated into chaos.

Cromwell's basic problem was thus a lack of civilian support: 'I am as much for a government by consent as any man, but where shall we find that consent?' (**19**). His reliance on the military was especially apparent at those times when his concern for security overrode his wish for consent. The rule of the Major Generals, in 1655–6, brought home the reality of the regime to Parliamentarian* squires who, since 1653, had begun to take part in local government again. Outsiders with a stern sense of duty, the Major Generals and their subordinates had little time for the favouritism and tempering of national requirements to local conditions which were a tradional feature of local government. 'Was I made a commissioner to do good or favour to my friends?' asked one officer. 'I never thought so, but to serve the state' (**34**). Such a centralised, authoritarian approach to government made that of the 1630s appear mild in retrospect. The later 1650s saw an increasing rapprochement between Royalists and Presbyterians. Men who had fought each other worked together in elections and Presbyterians corresponded with the exiled Charles II (**34, 93**).

If Cromwell's search for a political settlement failed, the army remained militarily invulnerable. Royalist plots and risings were betrayed or crushed (notably Sir George Booth's in 1659). Even after Cromwell died, on 3 September 1658, the army remained united. Oliver's son, Richard, succeeded him as Lord Protector. As he was a civilian, many Presbyterians hoped that his regime would be less dependent on the army. He called a Parliament early in 1659 which tried to restrict religious toleration and the political role of the army, but its conduct merely provoked the army, which forced Richard to dissolve it and recalled the Rump. The Rump still hated the army for dismissing it in 1653, but needed the army's military strength to make up for its lack of civilian support. The army needed the Rump to cover the nakedness of military rule with a cloak of spurious legitimacy and to vote the taxes without which the soldiers could not be paid. Their relationship was thus hardly a harmonious one, and the final break came on the issue of which was the dominant partner. The Rump insisted that it should control military appointments and promotions, the council of war disagreed, and on 13 October the Rump was expelled for the second time.

England thus reverted to direct military rule, but the committee of safety set up by the army faced great problems. The last of the taxes voted by the Rump would expire in December and there were many reports that people refused to pay taxes not voted by Parliament. The committee soon abandoned its threats to quarter soldiers on recalcitrant taxpayers, realising that this could provoke a general revolt. The City, restive and hostile, rejected requests for a loan. The judges refused to hear any more cases. Government was in danger of grinding to a halt and the regime was constantly reminded of its unpopularity. It tried to strengthen its support by creating a militia of sectaries, but this merely increased the resentment towards it and did not solve the basic problem of the need for a more permanent form of government. It was announced that a free government would be set up that was acceptable to all, but without a king or House of Lords. As the great majority of the political nation believed in monarchy, this was a contradiction in terms. By December it seemed that England was sliding into chaos.

The army leaders' problems were compounded by the conduct of General George Monk, an experienced professional soldier who commanded the army in Scotland. His competence as a soldier and military administrator is beyond doubt [**doc. 1**], but opinions varied as to his political abilities and the motives behind his conduct in 1659–60. Naturally, after the Restoration, he and his biographers (**13, 25**) claimed that he had intended, from the outset, to bring back the king, which would imply a political farsightedness of which there was later little sign: Pepys called him a blockhead. Indeed, if that was Monk's intention, it was far from obvious at the time: 'He is a black Monk and I cannot see through him', wrote one Royalist (**6**).

Many were confused by his capacity for saying one thing and doing another. It seems likely that he tried at all times to keep his options open and to cover himself against charges of acting without authority. Having served both king and republic, he probably lacked dogmatic attachment to any form of government, although he consistently stressed the need for order and authority in church and state. He was considering restoring the king in the summer of 1659. He wrote to Sir Anthony Ashley Cooper, a Presbyterian, that he wanted the Long Parliament recalled – in other words, as it had been before Pride's Purge, with a Presbyterian majority (**44**). He was in contact with Royalist emissaries at the time of Booth's rising and might have joined it had it not been defeated so quickly. Contacts with Presbyterians, Royalists and Rumpers continued in the autumn. A group of Presbyterian politicians, including the Earl of Manchester, tried to persuade him to bring back Charles II on the conditions offered to his father on the Isle of Wight in 1648, including stringent restrictions on the prerogative and a Presbyterian* system of church government. (Insofar as Monk expressed any views on religion, it would seem that he was a Presbyterian.)

Monk was stirred to political action by the growing confusion in England and by the interference of first the Rump, then the army leaders, in military appointments in Scotland. The Rump's expulsion gave him a pretext to take his stand on a defence of legally constituted authority and the superiority of the civil to the military power. He declared for a civilian government without king or Lords and for a settled godly ministry, began to purge his forces of officers whose loyalty was suspect, and prepared to march into England. As Monk's preparations would take some time, he embarked on tortuous negotiations with the English army leaders. While a force under Lambert watched the Scottish border, news of the disagreements between Monk and the grandees (as the army leaders were called) gave heart to the opposition to army rule, especially in London. Late in November Monk wrote to the lord mayor and common council, asking for their help in restoring Parliament to its former freedom – whether he meant the Rump or the Parliament of 1648 was unclear (**9, 23**). The City authorities responded warily, but the letter gave added force to the demand in London for a 'free Parliament' – perhaps a new, freely elected body, perhaps that of 1648. (Either would probably recall the king.)

Many soldiers looked to Monk, whose men were paid more regularly than they were. Some were confused by the divisions among their leaders and 'laid down their arms till they be satisfied for what and whom they engage' (**9**). By early December London was on the verge of anarchy. The army had to suppress several attempted risings. 'The soldiers here,' said a newsletter, 'are so vilified, scorned and hissed that they are ashamed to march' (**9**).

Caught between the citizens and the army, the City authorities side-stepped demands that they should petition for a free Parliament. The committee of safety fulminated that to promote such a petition was treason and bleated that Monk would bring back the king. It announced that a new Parliament (with tightly restricted powers) would meet on 24 January, but it was too late. Portsmouth's garrison declared for the Rump, as did a section of the fleet, which blockaded the Thames. The London common council elections saw a heavy defeat for the army's allies. The new common council called for a 'free Parliament' (although it could not agree what that meant) and demanded that the City should again organise its own militia, in the place of the militia of 'sectaries' which the army had tried to create. As the army's resolve crumbled, the Rump reconvened on 26 December. Major General Fleetwood told anyone who cared to listen that God had spat in his face.

The Rump proved as arrogant and vindictive as ever. Having voted the soldiers a month's pay, to keep them quiet, it began a purge of officers who had supported the committee of safety. It refused to admit some twenty-five MPs 'secluded' at Pride's Purge, unless they made a declaration against government by a single person or House of Lords; they refused. It revived an earlier plan to fill 'vacant' seats (including those of 'secluded' MPs) by holding elections, with stringent conditions to ensure that those elected would be politically acceptable to the Rumpers.

Despite its bravado, the Rump remained politically weak. It appointed a council of state to direct the government, but less than half its members would take an engagement to adhere to the republic. The call for a free Parliament could not be conjured away. Both Royalists and Presbyterians saw such a Parliament as the first step towards restoring the monarchy, even if they differed as to the terms on which it should be restored. Both had had their confidence boosted in December and had established a strong position in the City's government and militia, but if the City leaders refused to co-operate with the Rump, fear of the army made them reluctant to take a political stand. Everything thus depended on Monk [**doc. 2**] who on 1 January left his camp at Coldstream and marched into England.

As he headed south he was assailed from all sides with petitions, importunities and advice. Presbyterian peers and the City government sent emissaries, Royalists cultivated officers believed to be in his confidence, country gentry urged him to declare for a full, free Parliament, adding that they would pay no taxes until such a Parliament was called [**doc. 3**]. The Rump issued a declaration which tried to reconcile Monk's publicly stated concern for 'magistracy and ministry' with its desire to hang on to power [**doc. 4**]. Monk talked publicly of his unqualified support for the Rump, from which he derived authority; some who spoke to him privately believed he sympathised with the call for a free Parliament. The Rump, for its part, came to believe that he would do as he was told. Only his refusal to take the engagement (against government by a single person) and his advice to the Rump to hasten the elections it promised, without increasing the restrictions on future MPs, hinted at some disquiet on his part.

His loyalty to the Rump was soon put to the test. On 8 February the City common council resolved to pay no taxes until London's full complement of MPs was restored. Next day the Rump ordered Monk to take down the City's gates and the posts and chains across the streets and voted that the common council should be discontinued'. Monk duly had the posts and chains removed, but not the gates, saying that he was sure that the common council would rescind its vote if it were allowed to meet. The Rump was adamant: the gates were to be destroyed and a new common council elected, on a basis laid down by Parliament. It also resolved that the army should be governed by five commissioners, including Monk, of whom three should be a quorum. Hitherto Monk had acted by virtue of a commission as sole commander-in-chief, granted secretly by the Rump's previous council of state in November. Now he could be outvoted by the other commissioners.

It was the last straw. Already unhappy about the orders the Rump had given him, he demanded that the Rump should proceed at once to fill the vacant places by fresh elections, but instead of the Rump's proposal that (in effect) only republicans should be eligible, Monk insisted that membership should be open to all who had supported Parliament in the civil wars. This would lead to the installation of a moderate or Presbyterian majority, for the few sitting republicans would be heavily outnumbered by newly-elected moderates.

Ten days of complex manoeuvres followed. Monk remained in the City, despite the Rump's pleas that he return to Whitehall. The Rump, for its part, continued to insist on qualifications which would have debarred the majority of Parliamentarians* from participating in the forthcoming elections. Monk therefore moved towards a second method of filling up the Rump with moderates. On 21 February, guarded by Monk's troops, the MPs excluded in 1648 took their seats. Monk urged the enlarged Parliament to provide for a speedy dissolution and fresh elections for a new Parliament which, he said, 'may meet and act in freedom, for the more full establishing of this commonwealth, without a king, single person or House of Lords' (**23**).

In the following weeks Monk became more inscrutable than ever, but his conduct is not difficult to explain. He actions tended towards establishing a succession of Presbyterian Parliaments, which implied the restoration of the king, but on stringent conditions. When he asked Parliament, now with a Presbyterian majority, to settle 'such qualifications as may secure the public cause we are all engaged in', he must have expected these to exclude Royalists from voting or entering Parliament: that, certainly, is what happened. Parliament appointed a council of state, dominated by Presbyterians such as Ashley Cooper, Annesley and Holles. It sought to re-establish the short-lived Presbyterian church system of the 1640s (which had never won much support).

Monk was well aware that these moves would be deeply resented by the many republicans and religious radicals in the army. On the day the secluded MPs were restored, Monk and his officers issued a declaration in which they tried to assure the army that they would not betray all that it had fought for [**doc. 5**]. Monk also began a lengthy purge of the officer corps of the army and navy, while Parliament sought to create an alternative military force, a new militia commanded by Presbyterian, and sometimes Royalist, gentry. Monk dealt firmly with criticism of his conduct from within the army and demanded that the officers, and later the soldiers, should promise to submit to whatever should be decided by the next Parliament (**7**).

By the time Parliament dissolved itself on 16 March the question was not whether the king would be restored, but on what terms. The outgoing Parliament did all it could to ensure that those terms would favour the Presbyterians. The qualifications laid down for MPs excluded both Royalists and 'such persons that deny magistracy and ministry to be the ordinances of God' (**10**). If observed, these provisions would have ensured a Presbyterian majority, but public opinion moved so strongly in favour of monarchy that many Royalists were elected (**70, 71**).

Monk's role remained crucial, because he alone could control the army. As always, he moved cautiously, partly to avoid outraging the army (which was still being purged), partly because he wished to see how the elections turned out. Late in March he at last agreed to receive overtures from the king and opposed those Presbyterians on the council of state who sought to prescribe conditions for the king's return before Parliament met. As the election results showed the strength of Royalism and Monk refused to endorse their demands, individuals began to make their peace with the king.

Some Presbyterians were eager for office and in this found an unlikely ally. The Queen Mother, who had done so much to bring about her husband's downfall, sought to gain a similar ascendancy over her son. She and her English followers resented Charles's favour to his and his father's loyal servants, Edward Hyde, Edward Nicholas and the Marquis of Ormond. They made common cause with some Presbyterians who, with the French ambassador in London, schemed to persuade Charles to go from Brussels to Paris, where his mother could preside over the negotiations for his return. As a Catholic, she had no qualms about making concessions at the expense of the Church of England, or of the prerogative, provided these enabled her to exclude Hyde and his friends from power and establish her influence over her son.

These intrigues bore little fruit. Charles moved not to France but to Breda. In mid-April the French ambassador wrote that only Monk could prevent an unconditional restoration. The Presbyterians, baulked of their expected majority in the Commons, tried to exclude Royalists from the Lords on various pretexts and hoped to use their control of the Upper House to determine the terms of the king's return. They proposed to appoint a group of commissioners of the Great Seal, headed by Manchester, which would prevent Hyde's being made lord chancellor.

Their projects collapsed soon after the new Parliament, or 'Convention', met on 25 April. On 1 May the king's Declaration of Breda was read to the Commons, which referred to Parliament the contentious issues of Crown and Church lands, religious toleration and the punishment of the regicides, and promised to pay the army's arrears in full [**doc. 6**]. It was a shrewd document. It dealt with the points on which individuals had most need of reassurance and removed fears of indiscriminate royal vengeance, which were likely to impede the restoration. At the same time, it left open the question of the king's powers until after his return.

Early in May the Presbyterians tried several times to impose preconditions on the king. They proposed a committee of both Houses to order the militia and manage affairs of state, on the lines of the Committee of Both Kingdoms of the 1640s. They brought in bills to confirm sales of Crown and church lands, to grant toleration until a national synod could settle the church and to grant a general pardon. Monk promoted a package of measures which included some of these and in other ways went further [**doc. 7**]. Those close to Monk, notably William Morrice, soon to be made secretary of state, also urged Charles to accept conditions, but he saw no need to do so. There were too many bills before the Houses for any to stand much chance, especially in the face of Royalist obstruction [**doc. 12**]. Many Presbyterians reached private agreements with the king. 'There are none,' wrote the French ambassador sourly, 'who do not neglect the public interest in order to attend to their own private interests.'

On 8 May the king was formally proclaimed. As his return was now inevitable, it no longer seemed practical to seek to impose prior conditions, and the ambitious rushed to seek places and favours. The only bills presented to him on his arrival were to confirm the Convention's legality (in doubt, as it had not been summoned by a king) and to confirm the judicial proceedings of the last eighteen years (to prevent a free-for-all in the courts as litigants sought to reverse judgments against them). Other matters could be decided after the king's return.

When Charles landed at Dover on 26 May, and began a triumphal progress to London, England again had a form of government acceptable to the great majority of its people. For more than eleven years it had been ruled by narrow and often self-righteous cliques, dependent in the last analysis upon military force. These regimes were brought to an end by Monk, who neutralised the army, and by the sheer strength of the popular demand to bring back monarchy. From December 1659 this demand gathered momentum, especially in London. It disconcerted the army grandees, thwarted the Rump and persuaded Monk, probably reluctantly, that an unconditional restoration was unavoidable. When Charles returned the almost universal rejoicing reflected the national mood [**doc. 8, 9**]. Time was to show that he could not, or would not, fulfil the manifold and often contradictory expectations which his return aroused. For the moment, however, Royalists and Parliamentarians joined in welcoming him with a degree of unanimity and joy which had not been seen in living memory. As John Evelyn remarked, 'I stood in the Strand, and beheld it, and blessed God'.

2   The Restoration Settlement: The Convention

The Restoration settlement is often treated as the product of a rational process of bargaining between king and Parliament, in which each had clear-cut objectives. In fact, the legislation of 1660–4 was passed by two very different bodies, the Convention of 1660 and the 'Cavalier' Parliament elected early in 1661. Within each there were differences between Commons and Lords and various political and religious interests. Uncertainty abounded: for example, how much of the legislation passed since 1640 should remain in force? So many changes had been carried through by so many different bodies that MPs must have been unsure where to start.

As for the king, he was a stranger to his kingdom, with little first-hand knowledge of its institutions, of his leading subjects, and of the relative strengths of the political and religious groups which had emerged since 1640. He undoubtedly wished to consolidate his position, but probably had few clear ideas about how to do so and his councillors gave differing advice.

The settlement consisted of a series of *ad hoc* measures, which reflected not only the ebb and flow of politics but also, sometimes, misconceptions on the part of the king or politicians. And yet the legislation of 1660–4 created a viable basis for a lasting settlement. Piecemeal and untidy though it might be, it reflected a widely felt desire to return to the sort of ordered society and responsible monarchy which should have existed before the civil wars. This chapter and the next will consider the genesis of that legislation.

The Convention is among the most obscure of seventeenth-century Parliaments. It seems to have contained no clear-cut parties, the Commons dividing in different ways on different issues. A substantial proportion – maybe even half – of the Commons were men of Parliamentarian* backgrounds, but these were not united. Most were Presbyterians* – moderates who wanted a Puritan established Church – but a few were radical in politics or wanted a general toleration. Most wanted to restrict Charles's powers, to prevent him from abusing his authority as his father had done, and tried to rush through bills to that effect in the weeks before his return. Some, however, had achieved, or hoped for, office. These resisted attempts to curb the king's authority, either because they needed his favour or because such measures would restrict their own power as the king's servants. Thus Presbyterians like Annesley, Ashley Cooper or Morrice should normally be seen as supporters of the 'court'*, working on the king's behalf.

Ranged against the ex-Parliamentarians* were many MPs from Royalist backgrounds, elected despite the previous Parliament's efforts to declare them ineligible. By-elections and partisan decisions in election disputes increased their numbers as the year wore on. Despite complaints that these 'young men' did not attend assiduously, except for debates on religion, they were ably led by men like Sir Heneage Finch, while the Presbyterians became divided and disorganised. These MPs' Royalism did not necessarily make them co-operative. They resented Charles's lavish favour to Presbyterians, which owed something to Monk's influence and to the fear that they might cause trouble if they were not rewarded. They also watched suspiciously for any attempt to accommodate the Presbyterians within the Church of England (**70, 71, 80**). The net result of these confused alignments was that on many issues Parliamentarians* and Royalists cancelled each other out. The Convention achieved much in areas of broad agreement. It settled the most immediate problems left by the Interregnum and took the first steps towards making adequate financial provision for the Crown. On more contentious issues - the prerogative, the militia, the Church - the questions remained open, to be resolved by the Cavalier Parliament.

The First Session

The Convention's proceedings spanned two sessions, separated by a recess from 13 September to 6 November. The Houses merely adjourned over this period, so that bills unfinished in the first session could be taken up again in the second, but the nature of the sessions differed. The first was dominated by the legacies of the Interregnum. Matters relating to a long-term settlement were discussed, but had a low priority and major decisions were postponed. The second saw attempts to force decisions on the revenue, the militia and the Church. Meanwhile the political atmosphere at court was changing. In the summer Hyde and other Royalists broadly agreed with the Presbyterian councillors on the need to settle the problems left by the Interregnum, but by the autumn the court was becoming divided on questions of policies and personalities.

The Convention's most immediate problem was the indemnity. Many who facilitated Charles's return had made war on his father, so were liable to charges of treason. It would also be impossible to disband the army unless its members could be sure of immunity from prosecution for crimes committed while in arms. The Declaration of Breda had promised that Charles would assent to a general pardon, but left it to Parliament to decide who should be excluded from its benefits. Some, like Monk, urged that only a handful should forfeit their lives, although others might lose their estates. Many, Presbyterians as well as Royalists, wanted greater severity against both the regicides and the leading figures of the 1650s. Thus the Royalist Job Charlton

> moved against those that petitioned against the king or sat in Parliament between '48 and '49 and the high court of justice men and the contrivers of the Instrument [of Government] and the imposers of taxes under Oliver and major generals and decimators, and though he never pressed for the death of any, yet to secure the future peace of the kingdom he could not be silent.

Such measures against those involved in government in the 1650s (including a proposal that they be made to repay their salaries) would penalise men like Monk and Ashley Cooper, who had held office at that time, but not those Presbyterians, like Prynne, who had not. During days of ill-tempered wrangling, MPs gave vent to their vindictiveness while seeking to protect their friends and kinsmen. The Lords were, if anything, more vengeful, until Hyde persuaded them to moderate their demands. In its final form, the bill of indemnity excluded thirty men from pardon as to life or estate, but declared a general indemnity for all offences since 1637 and laid down penalties for maliciously raking up the past.

For Charles, the indemnity was politically essential. Until it passed, the army would not disband and the City would lend no money. It was also necessary to start to heal the divisions left by civil war, so that normal life could resume. He showed some impatience at the Houses' ghoulish bickering and, outwardly, urged 'mercy and indulgence'. Only occasionally was there a hint of the bitterness he must have felt, notably in his hounding of Sir Henry Vane (not a regicide) who was executed in 1662. In general, however, Charles suppressed his desire for revenge and gave his assent to the indemnity bill on 29 August.

A second problem created by the civil wars was that of land sales.

These were of three basic types. First, after the abolition of bishops in 1646 their lands were sold off, followed by those of deans and chapters*. Second, the lands confiscated from Royalist and Catholic 'delinquents' were first leased out and later sold. Third, most of the Crown's estates were sold off after the abolition of monarchy. The total income from these sales exceeded £6,000,000 (**33**), so many people had cause to fear financial loss when the king returned, including some whom the king wished not to upset, notably members of the army, the Presbyterian politicians who helped organise his return and City merchants, whose loans kept government going in these early months. The Declaration of Breda had referred the matter to Parliament. Monk proposed that most purchases of Crown and Church lands should be confirmed, with the purchasers paying a part of their annual value to the original owners, while Royalists should be able to regain their estates if they refunded the purchase price, plus interest [**doc. 7**].

The former proposal was made the basis of two bills, neither of which was passed. Although the king had referred the matter to Parliament, perhaps to avoid any firm commitment to the purchasers, it could not agree on what to do: the matter was too complex to be settled by general legislation, because individual circumstances varied so widely. Often tenants had bought land which they had formerly leased, or land was bought to be held in trust for its original owners. Sometimes Church lands and impropriated tithes* had been used to augment the income of a parish minister. Given such variation, many cases could be settled fairly only if considered on their particular merits.

The Convention's inability to resolve the matter left the initiative to others. The surveyor general began to resume possession of Crown lands in July, following an order from the Lords (never ratified by the Commons). Bishops and other ecclesiastics granted new leases as if they had never been deprived of their estates. In each case, compensation was negotiated individually with the purchasers, who often continued to lease the land which they had purchased. These improvised procedures were given greater consistency in October, when the king set up a commission of sales, to decide the compensation to be paid to purchasers of Crown and Church lands. Royalists and Catholics had to seek redress in the courts, but if their estates had been confiscated they were often successful. Only those who had sold land in order to pay fines had no hope of compensation.

For such a potentially contentious issue, the land question was settled remarkably amicably. One reason was that purchasers were allowed reasonable compensation, especially if they were politically influential, while some of the largest purchasers could not demand compensation, having lost their estates under the Act of Indemnity. Many, perhaps the majority, had recouped their investment before 1660, the lands having been sold comparatively cheaply. Where tenants had purchased land they formerly leased, it made little difference to them to revert to leasing, especially if the rent was moderate. Many Royalists and Catholics had regained their lands before 1660, through intermediaries. For these reasons the land settlement left little lasting rancour, except among the minority of Royalists who had lost heavily or recovered their lands at the price of a crushing burden of debt. Certainly, few influential purchasers had cause to complain (**64, 65, 111**).

The third immediate problem was to pay off the army and much of the navy; both contained many religious and political radicals and were expensive to maintain. Charles had promised at Breda to pay the officers and soldiers their arrears and to take them into his service on the same terms. The matter was, however, outside his control. He had no direct authority over the army, as Monk was commander-in-chief and the Convention took responsibility for paying the forces. All Charles could do was to raise the militia*, supplemented by gentlemen volunteers, to guard against any attempt by the army to re-establish a republic. That apart, he had to wait until Monk and the Convention saw fit to act. Monk took his time. Weeding out 'disaffected' officers was a slow business and he could demand favours, for himself and others, only so long as he remained the only man who could control the army.

By early July Charles had abandoned any thought of keeping up the army, and his spokesmen urged that it should be paid off quickly. They were supported by some Presbyterians who saw it as a threat to liberty [**doc. 16**]. The majority of the Commons, however, would not consider the army until the indemnity had been settled. Indeed, it was most unlikely that the army would disband peacefully until that had passed. Thereupon bills were passed to pay the soldiers' arrears and to allow them to practise trades as if they had completed an apprenticeship.

Together, these measures greatly eased the reabsorption of soldiers into civilian life. A committee of six peers and twelve MPs was set up to pay off the army, which proceeded slowly because of insufficient funds. Anxious forecasts that the army might, as in 1647, refuse to disband proved mistaken. This owed much to Monk's careful purges of the officer corps and to the care taken to satisfy the army's professional expectations. Changes in the upper ranks over the past year or two had weakened the bonds between officers and men and many soldiers were pressed men or fought purely for pay. The army had first become involved in politics because Parliament insensitively refused to settle its professional grievances: no such mistake was made in 1660. A few irreconcilable republicans plotted or went into exile, but most of the once formidable New Model disappeared quietly into civilian life.

Thus by the end of 1660 three of the thorniest problems created by the recent upheavals were well on the way to being resolved. On others, such as the constitution and religion, agreement was to prove more difficult.

The extent of the king's authority was, in 1660, open to argument. His power to raise revenue without Parliament's consent had been drastically reduced in 1641 by legislation to which Charles I had assented. He had also agreed to Acts taking away Star Chamber* and High Commission* and requiring Parliament to meet at least once every three years. Later he had been stripped of other powers without his consent, starting with his control of the militia*. After he left London early in 1642, the Long Parliament took over his executive functions, including the making of policy, the administration of justice and the raising and spending of money. Once the king had been defeated, a majority in Parliament was ready to lay down these responsibilities, provided he agreed to certain restrictions on his authority. Most MPs had no desire to govern the country, but wished to ensure that Charles should never again abuse his powers as he had in the 1630s. They demanded a share in the king's control of the armed forces and in his choice of advisers; he would concede neither, and deadlock ensued, until the abolition of monarchy made the question of the extent of the king's powers irrelevant.

The Convention had to consider how much of the legislation of the 1640s should stand and whether Charles should be pressed to agree to restrictions which his father had refused to concede. Before he returned, both Houses set up committees to consider the legislation passed since 1641, in order to decide which ordinances should be repealed: this implied that others should stand. Neither committee reported, but several bills were introduced which would substantially have restricted the king's power, by depriving him of his control over the executive and the militia* and his power to appoint officers of state and even members of his own household. It was also proposed that a series of bills should implement the promises in the

Declaration of Breda [**docs. 7, 11, 12**]. The bills failed because of Royalist obstruction and a simple lack of time. The declaration said nothing about the king's powers: he clearly wished to enjoy all those of his predecessors. Once he had returned without preconditions the bargaining position of those who wished to restrict his authority was weakened. They pinned their hopes on a bill to confirm the privileges of Parliament and the fundamental laws. After a leisurely progress through the Commons, who were preoccupied with the indemnity, this bill went up to the Lords on 3 July, where it stuck in committee,* despite reminders from the Commons.

The bill [**doc. 13**] set out a list of 'fundamental laws' to be confirmed. These included Magna Carta and the legislation of 1641 against Star Chamber*, High Commission* and Charles I's fiscal devices; there was no explicit mention of the Triennial Act*. There were two reasons why Charles should have disliked this bill. First, as later became clear, he wished to have some of the legislation of 1641 repealed. Second, the bill would confirm not only those statutes specified but all others for the defence of the privileges of Parliament and the liberties of the subject 'against arbitrary and illegal proceedings and taxes'. This could be construed to include some or all of the legislation of the Long Parliament and was probably intended to do so. There can be little doubt that the king used his influence in the Lords to block the bill. So long as it remained before the Lords' committee the Commons saw no need to put forward other proposals, so the question of the king's authority was left in suspense. From his point of view this was not unsatisfactory: at least he reserved his position.

There was a similar lack of resolution about the royal revenues until the end of the session. Initially the Convention, following the practice of the Long Parliament, kept the raising and spending of money in its own hands. The customs and excise* were renewed for short periods and a Commons' committee investigated arrears in the latter. Direct taxes on land (assessments) were voted for a few months at a time. The revenues designated to pay off the army were kept, not in the royal Exchequer, but in the Chamber of the City of London, and were paid out by a parliamentary committee. The Convention had no intention of abandoning its control of financial administration until the disbanding of the army was well advanced.

If some MPs hoped to use that control to extort concessions from the king, they failed to carry their colleagues. From the outset, the Convention accepted that he should have some revenues of his own. As most of the Crown's traditional revenues had been abolished or circumscribed in 1641, such a revenue would have to be granted by Paliament and this the Convention seemed willing to do. On 3 May the Commons ordered that a bill be brought in to abolish feudal tenures. This would confirm the abolition of wardship* by an ordinance of 1645, but whereas the king had received no compensation for the revenues abolished in 1641 he was now to receive £100,000 a year, from a tax on land.

The precise form of this compensation was not settled for another six months, during which the Commons moved slowly towards a permanent provision of revenue. On 19 June they voted to grant Charles the customs, tonnage and poundage, for life, as had been the practice over two centuries, with the single exception of Charles I. The Commons took some weeks to fix the rates on each commodity, but the Act received the royal assent on 28 July. It marked the first major step towards re-establishing the principle that the king should 'live of his own': that he should have a revenue for life, to support the cost of day-to-day government.

Earlier, Finch and the 'court'* element had blocked a proposal to set up a committee to regulate the excise*, so leaving the way open for the king to resume control of the administration of the revenue. The 'court'* also thwarted a move to make the grant of the customs conditional on the passage of the indemnity bill, the House stressing 'the entire confidence they have in His Majesty's goodness and relying on his royal word to pass the same afterwards' (**10**).

The 'court' did not get everything its own way. It failed to remove from the customs bill a clause that the duties specified 'and no other' were to be levied: there was to be no return to Charles I's impositions*. One who voted against the clause was the veteran Presbyterian, Denzil Holles, a vociferous opponent of Charles I's 'illegal' collection of import duties.

The grant of the customs did little to solve Charles's immediate financial problems. He had returned with little ready money, an expensive court to maintain and many calls on his generosity. This was the first revenue he received and on 29 August he claimed it had all gone towards paying off the army. Following his complaint a committee was set up to consider his revenue. Having considered figures for Charles I's revenue and expenditure, the House resolved without a division that the king needed a regular annual revenue of £1,200,000. It also accepted the committee's recommendation that bills be brought in to regulate the post office, the Crown lands and the sale of wine licences, with a view to maximising the income from these sources and so minimising the amount that would have to be raised by taxation. The House resolved to ask the king not to lease out royal estates too cheaply, or on long leases, a sensitive issue when he was inundated with petitions for such favourable treatment.

Quite how the figure of £1,200,000 was arrived at is uncertain, but there is no evidence that Charles thought it unsatisfactory. At this stage he and his financial officials can have had only the haziest idea of the true cost of the government or of the extent of its indebtedness, because so much routine financial business was still being handled by parliamentary committees. The fact that Finch was elected chairman of the committee suggests that the 'court'* was well represented there. Only time would show that the annual cost of government was greater than that estimated in 1660, and the problems which this created were exacerbated by the burden of debt left by the Restoration and by the initial failure of Charles's revenues to attain their expected yield (**42**). As far as his revenue was concerned, Charles must have felt, when the Convention adjourned, that a satisfactory settlement was not far off.

Questions of religion proved less tractable. The 1559 Church settlement initially pleased very few. For many committed Protestants, or Puritans*, the Church was 'but halfly reformed'. They wished to purge the Prayer Book services of their remaining 'Popish' elements and to place more emphasis on preaching and less on observance, more stress on improvisation and less on set forms. Having failed to persuade Elizabeth to change the official practice of the Church, many resorted to quiet nonconformity, omitting parts of the Prayer Book which they disliked.

In time the Puritans' militancy diminished. There were some parishes where the Prayer Book was used selectively, if at all, and where the minister and his lay allies tried to impose moral discipline on the less godly parishioners, but by James I's reign most people had become used to the Prayer Book. It had acquired the authority which, in a conservative society, came from habit. Its cycle of observances, like those of the Catholic Church, followed the farming year. Its emphasis on physical actions and set forms and prayers made it more accessible and comprehensible than Puritanism, with its more cerebral emphasis on the Word. While the Puritan minority continued to denounce the Prayer Book's imperfections, the 'silent majority' came to accept or to love it (**63, 94, 127**).

Most Puritans and many conformists were outraged by the conduct of Archbishop Laud. For Laud the Reformation had gone too far. It had reduced the stress on ritual and reverence which he saw as essential parts of Christian worship. It had undermined the clergy's spiritual authority over the laity. It had led to a cynical plundering of the Church's wealth and an unacceptable level of lay interference in its affairs. For Laud, it was vital for the clergy to reassert themselves, to insist that God should be worshipped, with due solemnity and reverence, in every parish church. In pursuing this goal, Laud had to contend both with Puritans, who regarded ceremonies as Popish, and with the boorish rusticity of many village communities, which saw nothing wrong with baptising babies in a bucket or dispensing communion wine in an ale tankard. Over the years, most parish clergymen had learned to accept that neither their churches nor their parishioners could be brought to perfection. Church buildings were all too often dilapidated and dirty. Many villagers had little understanding of religion (not too surprisingly, given their lack of education) and allowed their dogs and children to wander at will during services. Laud refused to compromise with human imperfection and sought to impose his own, impossibly high standards on the whole Church. In so doing he provoked to anger many who, in general, had no quarrel with the Church's government and worship and opened the way for a radical Puritan minority to press for the thorough reformation which they had always demanded. Only drastic changes, they claimed, starting with the abolition of bishops, could cleanse the Church of the ills of Laudianism and Popery. Thus in bringing down Laud they hoped also to bring down the existing Church of England.

In 1640–2 most of those who loved the Prayer Book but resented Laudian innovation were confused and demoralised: they wanted to return to the way things had been under Elizabeth and James I, but did not know how. The radicals seized their chance. For generations most educated Protestants had believed in the prophecies of Daniel and Revelation and pondered over their precise meaning. The religious wars of this period were seen as the last great struggle between Christ and Antichrist, which would end with the defeat of the latter. This would be followed by the rule of the saints, who would prepare for Christ's Second Coming, the Day of Judgment and the end of the world. Laud's downfall seemed to many to usher in the rule of the saints. (**85**). Exhortations to godly reform abounded. Little groups of self-styled saints began to meet to seek God in a purer and holier way, untainted by the sinful majority. The tendency towards separatism had long been apparent but had been held in check. Now the Church's authority collapsed, opening the way to debate and experiment.

The 'gathered churches' of the 1640s had by 1660 hardened into sects, each with its own doctrines, organisation and sense of identity: Independents (or Congregationalists), Baptists, Quakers. All agreed that they should be free to worship in their own way and rejected the idea of a national church in which saints and sinners mingled indiscriminately.

For the great majority of Protestants, however, a single, uniform church was necessary for the maintenance of an ordered Christian polity, a belief confirmed by what most saw as the heretical, immoral and subversive conduct of the Ranters, Quakers and other extreme sectaries. Until the rise of Laud, most people had found the Church of England quite satisfactory, doctrinally and liturgically. Any hope of simply reforming Laudian episcopacy was killed by Charles's intransigence and by Parliament's need to seek Scottish military aid. The Scots Presbyterian clergy insisted that the price of that aid had to be the abolition of bishops in England.

This created serious problems for those who had no quarrel with episcopacy and who would have been content had Charles I's Church been run by men like Jewel or Grindal. Forced by circumstances beyond their control to abolish episcopacy, they found it difficult to establish anything else in its place. Scotland offered an obvious model, but few laymen wanted a system which would give so much power to the clergy. Since the Reformation, laymen had come to dominate many areas of English religious life. They legislated for the Church in Parliament, appointed well over half the parish clergy and collected many ecclesiastical revenues for their own profit.

Parliament therefore created a system in which the clergy were subordinated to lay elders. It aroused little enthusiasm (and some hostility) in most parts of the country and soon lost even the support of the central government when the Presbyterians lost power in Pride's Purge. Later hopes that Oliver or Richard Cromwell might establish an effective, ordered, non-episcopal church proved illusory.

Once it was clear that monarchy would be restored, most assumed that a national church would be restored with it. Such a church was as much a part of the 'old regime' as the monarchy, and Charles I had, in sense, died for the Church of England. Moreover, as Dr Morrill has shown, there was a strong attachment to Anglican practice which successive Puritan regimes had been unable to break: attempts to prohibit the celebration of Christmas, for example, had proved an abject failure (**94**).

If the Church was to be restored, two questions had to be answered. First, what sort of Church? Should it be Anglican, based on the 1559 Prayer Book and so acceptable to a broad spectrum of moderate conformists, or a more 'Puritan' Church, with concessions to the Presbyterians? Second, should the sects which had emerged since 1640 be allowed to worship freely or should the machinery of the law be used to force them to conform to the established Church? Thus the Church settlement hinged on the related, but separate, questions of comprehension and indulgence.

The fact that the Anglican Church was eventually restored, without concessions to the Presbyterians or toleration for Dissenters, should not lead us to assume either that it was obvious from the start that this would happen, or that Charles and Hyde wished it to happen (**39**). Such a view relies too much on the hindsight of men like Richard Baxter, as they tried to explain the dashing of their high hopes of 1660 (**1**). It also takes on trust Hyde's later claim that he unswervingly promoted the Church's interests, a claim coloured by his later role as champion of intransigent Anglicanism (**8**). The reality was more complex and obscure.

Charles's own religious views are hard to pin down, not least because of his deceitfulness. He had a lively, if idiosyncratic, interest in theology, but had little time for formal worship or sermons. Given a free choice, he would probably have preferred Catholicism to anything else and he became a Catholic on his deathbed, but that did not stop him conforming to the Church of England until his last hours, or ruthlessly sacrificing the lives and property of innocent Catholics when that was politically necessary. His approach to religion was essentially political. His grandfather, Henry IV of France, had become a Catholic in order to secure his crown; Charles conformed to the established Church in order to retain his. In 1660, the form of that church had not yet been decided. Charles's first impression must have been that Presbyterianism was very strong, an impression which Monk and the Presbyterian councillors did all they could to reinforce. By contrast, the Church of England was institutionally decayed, few of the bishops were still alive and there was little sign yet of the strength of Anglican sentiment. Prudence therefore seemed to suggest that the Presbyterians should be accommodated within the restored national Church.

It seems, however, that Charles's commitment to comprehension went beyond short-term political calculation, for he persisted in trying to give the Presbyterians some satisfaction long after the strength of Anglicanism had become apparent. He may simply have been slow to recognise that strength, but there was also another explanation. He was only too aware that his restoration owed little to his own efforts. A sudden shift of opinion had brought him home: another could send him on his travels again. He had no love for Presbyterianism: he had not forgotten how the Scots clergy had forced him to denounce the sins of his parents in 1650 as the price of military aid. As with the indemnity, however, the need for reconciliation and for a broad basis of support overcame his repugnance at making concessions to his family's former enemies. Throughout 1660 he tried, apparently sincerely, to re-establish the Church in a form acceptable to the Presbyterians. Hyde's role is more problematical, not least because he later tried to obscure it. He believed that an episcopal Church should be restored as part of the traditional constitutional structure and as a means of maintaining ecclesiastical order and decency, but that was not incompatible with comprehension. The majority of Presbyterians would work within an episcopal Church, provided the bishops' power was curtailed. The pernickety Baxter approved almost without demur a scheme of 'limited episcopacy' drawn up by archbishop Ussher of Armagh. Some of Hyde's allies among the clergy, notably George Morley, wished to bring the Presbyterians into the Church. It seems likely that Hyde also worked for comprehension in 1660, either because he thought it desirable or because he was following Charles's orders.

The first problem facing king and Convention was that of the parish clergy. Many Anglicans had been deprived of their livings in the 1640s, for Royalism or 'scandalous' conduct. Of those in livings in 1660, most had been ordained by bishops, but some had been ordained under the Presbyterian system. There were a few of extreme views, but the great majority were either Presbyterians or Anglicans who had conformed in the 1650s: indeed, the line between the two was not easy to draw. When Charles returned, the ejected clergy hoped to regain their livings, while those in possession wished to keep them. On 9 May a bill was brought in to secure the latter, but it had not passed by the time Charles returned. He found himself in an awkward position. He could not simply reject the claims of clergymen who had lost their livings because of their loyalty to his father's Church, but he was unwilling to alienate the Presbyterian clergy and politicians.

Three days after reaching London Charles issued a proclamation that no incumbent should be removed except by due process of law or order of Parliament. His aim was to prevent ejected ministers from regaining possession by force while Parliament was still considering the matter. In September an Act of Parliament decreed that ejected ministers should be restored, provided they compensated those they supplanted, but confirmed all other ministers in possession, except for the few who had petitioned for the king's death, actively opposed the Restoration or denied the validity of infant baptism.

Royalist MPs pressed for more stringent doctrinal tests, but were defeated, perhaps because the king used his influence against them: the appointments which Charles and Hyde now made to vacant benefices, mostly of men who had held livings in the 1650s, do not suggest a commitment to rigid Anglicanism. Hyde also helped to thwart an attempt by Royalists to recover impropriated tithes* confiscated in the 1640s; some had been used to augment the income of parish ministers, an achievement which many Presbyterians wished to preserve. There was inevitably some disruption in 1660: ministers were ejected or reinstated in maybe 700 of England's 9,000 or so parishes, but in many cases Charles and Hyde reconciled the various conflicting interests (**64**).

Settling the Church's government and liturgy was more difficult, but less urgent. While the Declaration of Breda talked only of liberty to 'tender consciences', Charles had written at the same time to the Speaker of the Commons promising to propose, in due course, 'somewhat for the propagation' of the Protestant religion (**10**). Monk wrote of the need to call a synod of divines to settle religion, in conjunction with Parliament [**doc. 7**].

For the Presbyterians, three main points were at issue. First, Church government: they would agree to the restoration of episcopacy only if the bishops consulted with representatives of the parish clergy, as in Ussher's scheme (**38**). Second, they wished to be allowed to omit features of the Prayer-Book services which they thought unnecessary or Popish, such as kneeling for communion, wearing a surplice or using the sign of the cross in baptism. Third, they wanted Presbyterian ordinations to be treated as valid, while Anglicans claimed that since only a bishop could ordain a priest, those ordained by presbyters should be reordained. The third demand was a product of the 1640s and 1650s, but the other two repeated Puritan demands for further reform going back to Elizabeth's reign.

Some Presbyterian ministers who waited on Charles at Breda came away convinced that he favoured comprehension, but he was in no hurry. Some of his emissaries supported the idea of a national synod, but that might have been seen as a way to delay any decision until more urgent matters, like the indemnity and disbanding the army, had been settled. It is unlikely that Charles welcomed a bill brought into the Commons on 27 June 'for the maintenance of the true reformed Protestant religion'. In a series of often ill-tempered debates in committee*, some Anglicans argued that the Thirty-Nine Articles, and not just the Bible, defined the doctrine for the established Church; others claimed the bill was unnecessary, as the legislation which established the Church had never lawfully been repealed. The House eventually accepted the proposal of 'court'* spokesmen, both Anglican and Presbyterian, to ask the king to call a national synod and to adjourn the debate until 23 October [**doc. 14**]. This left the way open for Charles to arrange a settlement which avoided the entrenched positions revealed in these debates and rested on his prerogative rather than an Act of Parliament. When Parliament adjourned in September, Hyde announced that the king would soon publish a declaration granting indulgence to those who differed from their brethren for reasons of conscience. The same day Nicholas wrote that now Parliament had adjourned the king could think about the church settlement.

The Second Session

During the recess the rough consensus at court began to break down. The Presbyterian councillors may not have liked Hyde, but worked with him because he was secure in Charles's favour and the king was eager to conciliate them. Charles saw Hyde as the architect of his restoration and as a willing workhorse, ready to deal with the administration which Charles found so tedious and with the petitions which flooded in. Hyde's solemn haughty manner and the favour he enjoyed had made him enemies over the years, notably the queen mother's followers and some younger, more frivolous courtiers, but in the summer of 1660 his position seemed impregnable.

By the autumn, things were changing. On 3 September the king's brother, James, Duke of York, secretly married Hyde's daughter, who was pregnant by him. James soon had second thoughts and many at court argued that such an unequal match should not be allowed to stand: Hyde came of a modest gentry background, and some alleged that he was scheming to place his grandchildren on the throne. (Charles was as yet unmarried, so James was his heir-presumptive.) Charles was furious, not with Hyde, but with his brother. Although he rejected suggestions (not least from his mother) that he should have the marriage annulled by Act of Parliament, the episode convinced Hyde's enemies that he could be toppled and made Hyde work harder at maintaining the king's favour. This was shown clearly during the recess by the part he played in negotiating a church settlement.

After informal discussions with Presbyterian ministers, Hyde drew up (by 4 September) a draft of the declaration to which he referred at the adjournment. Some expressions in it displeased the Presbyterians: those favouring ceremonies, he wrote, were 'much superior in number and quality' to those who did not. Charles called the draft 'a strange pottage' and a group of Presbyterian councillors and divines drew up papers of objections. On 22 October each article of a revised draft was discussed at a conference at Hyde's London home, Worcester House. Most of the discussion concerned comprehension, but Hyde also proposed 'that others also may be permitted to meet for religious worship' provided they did not disturb the peace. Baxter protested that this might allow liberty to Papists (although he was just as intolerant of Quakers or Baptists) and the matter was dropped (**1, 32, 64**). Next day the king ordered two of the more moderate bishops to meet with the Presbyterian divines Calamy and Reynolds, and with Holles and Annesley, to try to reach agreement on reordination.

On 25 October the Worcester House Declaration was published. It avoided questions of theological right and wrong, and argued pragmatically the need for peace and order, for a single Protestant church to guard against Popery and for the subordination of the ecclesiastical to the civil power. It avoided the vexed point of reordination, but on other matters gave the Presbyterians much of what they wanted. Bishops were to be asisted by suffragans and rural deans. The parish clergy were to have much more power to exclude errant parishioners from communion, which would make them better able to impose moral discipline. Revision of the Prayer Book was to be referred to a synod containing equal numbers of Anglicans and Presbyterians, but meanwhile incumbents could omit ceremonies or parts of the Prayer Book which were against their consciences [**doc. 15**].

It has been claimed that this Declaration was a ruse to lull the Presbyterians until they could be crushed by a more Anglican Parliament (**39**). This seems most implausible. The trend of Charles's religious policy in 1660 was consistently towards accommodation with the Presbyterians. He delayed appointing new bishops and when he did (August) he offered bishoprics to three Presbyterians (Calamy, Reynolds and Baxter) and told the French ambassador he thought they would accept. His motives were political: he was not inhibited by a spiritual or emotional attachment to Anglicanism.

Meanwhile, a second strand of policy began to emerge. However broad the established Church might be, there would be many outside it. These included the sectaries, numerous enough to cause trouble if provoked, and the Catholics, who had served the Stuarts well and for whom Charles had considerable sympathy. These could not be brought within the Church, but they could be granted the indulgence promised at Breda. That promise (drafted by Hyde) had been restricted to those who 'do not disturb the peace of the kingdom', which to Hyde ruled out most of the sects and probably the Catholics. Thus when he proposed on 22 October that 'others' should be able to worship freely, he was probably acting on orders: Charles's waspish reply to Baxter's remarks about the Papists showed where his sympathies lay.

In a revealing letter of 23 October, Bishop Morley wrote that he was eager to have the Worcester House Declaration published

> which I hope will give abundant satisfaction to the honest and peaceably minded men of both parties, and make them cease to be parties any longer, but unanimously to join against the common enemy, the Papists, who will grow much more insolent than ever they were if somewhat be not quickly done to prevent it; for the queen will be in England on Monday, which will be a great countenance and encouragement to them (**17**).

The reference to the queen mother's imminent arrival helps explain Hyde's behaviour. Dr Green has argued persuasively that Hyde had little enthusiasm for the Declaration but was acting on orders. His absence (and Baxter's) from the meeting called on the 23rd is significant: both were likely to hinder agreement (**64**). Well aware that his daughter's marriage had shaken his standing at court, Hyde was in no position to defy the king. Charles had every reason to feel satisfied. The Declaration was generally welcomed by Presbyterians and the Anglicans were as yet too disorganised to offer much protest. As the settlement outlined in the Declaration rested on his authority, not Parliament's, it could be modified if need arose. Nicholas wrote that the king had taken the most contentious issue (Church government) into his own hands, so could hope for a successful session of Parliament (**4**).

The Commons, on reassembling, resolved to thank the king for the Declaration and voted to bring in a bill to implement its provisions. This was not to the king's liking and he managed to get it rejected by 26 votes on 28 November. The debates give no indication of the position of the 'court'* Presbyterians, except Morrice, who was against the bill. The Anglicans were solidly against it and they were supported by the few Independents in the House. The king thus prevented a definite decision and kept his options open.

On two matters he did want a clear-cut decision. One was the militia,* the only regular military force in early Stuart England, as there was no standing army. Charles I had not agreed to the militia ordinance of 1642 and his son acted as if he possessed all his predecessors' powers over the militia, powers which rested on the Statute of Winchester of 1285. A week after his return he was issuing commissions to lords lieutenant and deputies in the traditional way. Given the army's uncertain loyalty and the danger of popular disaffection, he needed a military force which, unlike the army, was under his own command. Many ex-Royalists were eager to have arms in their hands to guard against, or to harass, those they saw as 'disaffected': hence the creation of bands of gentlemen volunteers alongside the militia.

Some militia officers were over-zealous, to say the least. By November stories abounded of acts of petty tyranny, including arbitrary imprisonment of the supposedly disaffected, conduct made more unpalatable by uncertainty about the legality of the officers' authority, the militia ordinance having been neither repealed nor declared null and void. In November and December the Commons debated the militia several times. Some Presbyterians like Marvell believed it was necessary to regulate the militia in order to protect the subject against abuses of authority, but when a bill to that effect was put before the Commons, they bitterly denounced the form in which it was cast. They claimed that it would establish martial law and could lead to a regime like that of Cromwell's Major Generals. Many were not 'forward to confirm such perpetual and exorbitant powers by a law' (**21**) and despite the efforts of Finch and other 'court' spokesmen, the bill did not pass (**70**).

The other outstanding issue was the revenue. The Presbyterians tried to delay matters, hoping to use the financial weapon to force the king to allow the Worcester House bill to pass. Slowly the 'court'* wore them down. The bill abolishing feudal tenures passed at last, but the king's compensation was now to be half the excise rather than £100,000 a year on land. This change reflected not so much a wish to shift the burden from land to the consumer as an inability to agree how to apportion the load and a feeling that, with a six months' assessment voted to pay off the army, land was already paying more than its fair share. Whatever the reason for the change, calculations that half the excise would be worth more than £100,000 a year proved correct.

Later, after voting by a majority of two not to grant the king the other half of the excise, the House changed its mind, despite pleas that the yield of the king's revenues should be investigated first. Charles believed that the excise would take his annual revenue well above £1,200,000, which shows how badly informed he and his financial officials were. Despite all the Presbyterians' efforts to delay it (especially after the Worcester House bill was rejected) the excise bill had passed all its stages when the Convention was dissolved on 29 December.

Charles had announced the coming dissolution on 20 November. His decision to bring the Convention to an end can have had nothing to do with the vote not to grant the second half of the excise, which was on the 21st. The most likely reason was that given by the Venetian resident – the 'unquiet spirit' of the Commons, especially on religion. Charles may also have resented the vehement criticism of the lords lieutenant and of the militia bill.

Even so, he cannot have been too dissatisfied with the Convention's record. It had settled the problems of indemnity, disbanding and land sales and had gone a long way towards providing an adequate revenue. Its attempts to limit his prerogatives and to turn his Declaration into a bill had been thwarted. If it had not passed the militia bill, it had not challenged his right to control the militia. There is little evidence that he was planning to abandon the Presbyterians. The day he announced his decision to dissolve Parliament he promoted three Presbyterian lawyers. All the signs were, wrote one of the queen mother's servants, that the monarchy would be re-established 'at the highest point that has ever been'. There was every reason to expect the next Parliament to continue in similar vein.

3   The Restoration Settlement: The Cavalier Parliament

The last weeks of 1660 saw signs of major political change. The months since the king's return had been a time of moderation and reconciliation. The even balance within the Convention prevented the adoption of extreme measures. At court Clarendon co-operated with the Presbyterians because the king insisted on conciliation. In the provinces the Royalist gentry took time to regain confidence and to establish themselves in office, while the radicals lay low and the army disbanded quietly.

By November, however, complaints that Royalist officials were harassing Parliamentarians* and sectaries. Plots in December and Venner's rising in January created great alarm, an alarm sustained by rumours of risings over the next few years. These rumours increased the vindictiveness of local Royalists and they tried to crush completely the remnants of the 'good old cause'.

This Cavalier backlash found expression in the strongly Royalist House of Commons elected early in 1661. Whereas in the Convention Presbyterians and Royalists largely cancelled each other out, with the latter dominant much more partisan measures were likely. The king could no longer play one faction off against the other, but this would create few problems provided the Royalist majority approved of his conduct of government. If not, MP's Royalism would not inhibit them from defying him or from trying to impose their will upon him.

The polarisation in the provinces, with the counterpoint of Cavalier repression and radical plotting, evoked an ambivalent response from the king's government. On one hand, Charles still tried to conciliate the Presbyterians and the sects. On the other, he tried to extend his authority and powers of coercion, both as an end in itself and as a means of coping with sedition.

The tension between conciliation and repression was heightened by growing factional divisions at court. The ascendancy of Hyde, created Earl of Clarendon in April 1661, was first shaken by the scandal surrounding his daughter's marriage. Fear that the queen mother might re-establish her influence led him to work more closely with the Presbyterians: in November 1660 it was remarked that they depended on his favour (**15**). With the election of the Cavalier Parliament, the Presbyterians' usefulness to the king decreased: no longer would 'court'* Presbyterians play a vital part in managing Parliament. In September 1661 the French ambassador wrote that Charles could have abandoned the Presbyterians some time before, but had decided not to do so for the moment. While their influence subsisted, they gave support to Clarendon in his opposition to violent methods and his preference for caution and legality. 'The men are impatient to have all done at once,' he remarked on one occasion, 'but it must be done by degrees' (**4**).

Clarendon's caution left him open to accusations of lack of zeal for the king's service. His most outspoken critic was the Earl of Bristol. Debarred from office by his Catholicism, he was active in court intrigue and took the lead in alleging that Clarendon had deliberately neglected opportunities to maximise the royal revenue and to establish a standing army [**doc. 17**]. In fact, close examination of the behaviour of the Convention and Cavalier Parliament suggests that neither body was likely to enhance the king's powers nearly as much as Clarendon's critics claimed.

As time went on, Charles's original strategy of conciliation became identified with Clarendon, his old Royalist friends like Nicholas and Southampton, and the Presbyterians. Their rivals advocated a more aggressive, authoritarian approach.

Apart from Bristol, Clarendon's leading critic was Sir Henry Bennet. Like Bristol he had been no friend of Hyde's in exile and on returning to England in April 1661 he used his courtly charm to insinuate himself into Charles's favour. The criticisms which he and Bristol made were echoed by those courtiers whom Clarendon called 'the little people', who amused the king by mocking the pompous chancellor. They found patrons in the king's mistress, Lady Castlemaine, and, after her return in 1662, the queen mother. Their first major success came in October 1662 when Bennet superseded Nicholas as secretary of state.

Throughout, Bennet and Bristol exploited Charles's irritation with the lectures Clarendon gave him. Their talk of strengthening the monarchy appealed to an essentially insecure king and they were ready – in Bristol's case, eager – to try to improve the position of the Catholics. It would be misleading to see concern for Catholicism as the key to Charles's policies – he did not feel that strongly about *any* religion and always put self-preservation first – but he inclined towards Catholicism and felt Catholics had long been harshly treated, so favoured the repeal of some of the more draconian laws against them.

This put Clarendon in an awkward position. Less rabidly anti-Catholic than most of his contemporaries, he thought it unwise to favour them too openly. The Anglicans would resent it and it would be harder to grant relief to Protestant Disssenters if it was linked to indulgence to Catholics. Moreover, if the laws against Catholics' holding office were removed, Bristol and other court Catholics would gain in influence. As the king ordered him not to oppose moves to help the Catholics, Clarendon had to obey, but his compliance did him little good as he was accused of stirring up trouble underhand (**64, 90**).

Such assaults on his position distressed him. He wrote to Ormond in September 1662

> The worst is, the king is as discomposed as ever and looks as little after his business, which breaks my heart and makes me and other of your friends weary of our lives. He seeks for his satisfaction and delight in other company, which do not love him as well as you and I do (**17**).

Rumours that he would be dismissed proved premature. Charles was too astute to deprive himself of a loyal, hardworking servant or to place all his reliance on one faction, however amusing it might be. An attempt by Bristol to impeach Clarendon in 1663 failed ludicrously. Even so, Charles relied more on Bennet and Bristol as time went on, especially when Clarendon was prostrated by gout.

The factionalism at court, the unwise policies of Bennet and Bristol and their inept attempts at parliamentary management together soured the relationship of king and Parliament. The Commons might be strongly Royalist, but would not submit tamely to whatever the king chose to do. They expected frugal and honest government, firm measures against political and religious dissidents and uncompromising Anglicanism. Charles satisified none of these expectations. Most Royalists felt that Parliamentarians* had received too many favours and there were many complaints about the court's corruption and rapacity.

This groundswell of dissatisfaction encouraged politicianss to carry their feuds into the Commons, initiating attacks on the alleged misdeeds of their rivals. In 1663 there were investigations into sales of offices (especially to Parliamentarians*) and into the management of the revenue: Clarendon's friend Southampton was lord treasurer and they had many clients in the revenue administration.

The French ambassador wrote that Charles's ministers were so eager to destroy each other that the sky could fall without their noticing. Bennet and Bristol also claimed that they could manage Parliament more efficiently than Clarendon, who relied on informal chats with his old cronies. Bennet argued the need for careful canvassing and systematic distribution of rewards, but there was a major row when it was alleged that Bristol's ally, Sir Richard Temple, had 'undertaken' to manage the Commons. In fact, such management could work only if most MPs approved of the king's policies, especially on religion. Bennet and his friends blamed Clarendon for the essentially spontaneous opposition to the king's ecclesiastical policy. He, for his part, denounced Bennet's 'weak and unskilful' management. Like Morrice and many others, he felt that 'if we do not commit great faults ... that body will serve the crown to a degree none ever did'.

The Cavalier Parliament was as loyal as any Charles was likely to find. It was more willing than the Convention to enhance his authority, but not to the point where it could threaten the liberty and property of the Anglican gentry. MPs were willing and eager to abandon the executive role which Parliament had taken up in the 1640s and which the Convention continued, at least in disbanding the army. Such a role involved too much time and effort. Most MPs had no wish to be professional politicians or administrators. Few received wages and to stay in London was expensive and sometimes unhealthy. Most were country squires, whose roots lay in their counties. Merchants and lawyers had businesses and practices to run. Parliament's assumption of a major role in government had been the product of exceptional circumstances, which no longer applied. They wished to return to normality, which meant government by the king, his councillors and officials. Those ambitious for government office could seek it in the king's service.

Not only did the Cavalier House of Commons want the king to govern, they wanted him to govern effectively. Until 1640, the main threat to the constitutional and ecclesiastical order had seemed to come from above, from Charles I and Laud, from 'Popery and arbitrary government'. From 1640 it became clear that they could also be threatened from below, by political and religious radicals and by popular involvement in politics, which the gentry and urban elites had always regarded as their exclusive preserve. There was thus support for measures that would make the king better able to hold down these disruptive forces, but not for any which might allow him to construct the sort of quasi-absolutist regime which seemed to be developing in the 1630s. Vengeful Royalists, in Parliament and the provinces, were all in favour of measures which allowed them to persecute their former enemies, but had little time for any which might allow the king to oppress *them*; they were especially wary of a standing army. While allowing the king to resume control of the executive and providing a revenue sufficient (on paper) to support his government, they would not give so much that he could do without Parliament. They did not want Parliament to govern; they wanted it to meet regularly to scrutinise and criticise the king's conduct of government and wished the king to be sufficiently in need of money for its criticisms to be heeded. Despite its Royalism, the Cavalier Parliament could not be taken for granted, as was clearly seen in its early years (**86**).

Security and the Machinery of Coercion

Rumours of plots and Venner's rising led to orders to call out the militia, to search the houses of suspect persons for arms, to break up conventicles* and to imprison those who stirred up sedition. These orders were often obeyed with excessive enthusiasm: a proclamation was issued against searching houses without a warrant.

Concerned for his safety Charles raised a regiment of foot and another of horse; the cost of these, and of his life guards, was to be met by disbanding garrisons in inland towns. By March 1661 the alarm had subsided, but Charles was still nervous. When Parliament met in May, he urged the Houses to confirm the Act of Indemnity, but also to deal severely with those who still acted on republican principles.

This showed the tension between his earlier concern for conciliation and a newer emphasis on authority and repression. On one hand, he still sought a broad Church settlement, perhaps supplemented by a measure of toleration, and tried to restrain the more extravagant Royalists: the Earl of Derby was summoned to London to explain his refusal to accept non-Royalists as deputy lieutenants* in Lancashire. On the other hand, fear of plots led to orders to arrest and imprison suspicious persons. Late in 1662 half a dozen alleged plotters were hanged to show that they had been involved in conspiracy and only Clarendon's legal scruples prevented others being sent to Louis XIV's galleys. Above all, Charles sought to strengthen his means of coercion, the militia* and the army.

The first major move against 'disaffection' owed more to the Commons than to the king and showed their differing priorities. In

June 1661 a bill was brought into the Commons to regulate municipal corporations. Whereas the king appointed county magistrates and officials, most towns elected their own. In the 1640s many Royalists were ejected from municipal office. Since the king's return some Royalists had been reinstated, often at the king's request, and their Parliamentarian* replacements removed, but many 'disaffected' men remained in office. The Commons proposed to appoint commissioners to remove such men and install 'well-affected' persons in their place. The Lords wished to replace this plan for a purge with one to give the king sweeping powers to appoint key officials. Boroughs were to be forced to take out new charters (presumably restricting their autonomy) and to lose their independence of the county JPs.*

The Commons were indignant. Their bill would purge disaffected members of corporations without destroying the towns' privileges and autonomy, as the Lords' amendments would [**doc. 18**]. They rejected the amendments without a division. When the matter was raised again after the summer recess, the Lords accepted what was, in substance, the Commons' original bill (**87**). It seems clear that the initiative for the bill came from the Commons and that the Lords' amendments expressed the wishes of the court*.

As things turned out, the Commons must have been well satisfied. The commissioners appointed under the Act did their job thoroughly. They had the power to remove anyone who refused to take the oaths of allegiance and supremacy, an oath against resisting the Crown and a declaration against the Covenant. They could even remove anyone who had satisfied these conditions whom they still considered 'disaffected'. They were then to fill vacant places as they judged fit. Although some, like the Earl of Derby, thought the commissioners were not rigorous enough, they implemented changes more sweeping than any of the previous twenty years, much to the Cavaliers' satisfaction. The king seems to have had reservations at first about the wisdom of embarking on a purge – hence the Lords' amendments. He must have been well pleased when the purge was carried through without serious disturbance.

For Charles, removing the 'disaffected' from corporations was less important than strengthening his military resources. In the spring of 1661 he had only three regiments of guards and his control of the militia* lacked a statutory basis. He clearly expected Parliament to make the militia more serviceable. In July it passed a bill stating that the king alone should direct the militia, but it took longer to lay down the precise form of that militia. In December the Commons heard of a plot to seize deputy lieutenants* in Lancashire and a committee was set up to consider how to make the militia more effective.

Clarendon then proposed a committee of both Houses to investigate the alleged plot over the Christmas recess and to consider proposals for a professional force, at least on a temporary basis, so that the militia need not be constantly on duty. Many saw in this a design to establish a standing army, under the Duke of York. Taken aback by this reaction, Clarendon referred the whole matter back to Parliament. After much debate, the Commons resolved to raise a temporary auxiliary force of 1,200, out of the militia, but even this project for a more professional 'select militia' was later dropped.

Instead, the Commons resolved that the militia should continue as it was, but that the king should have the power to raise up to £70,000 a year for three years, through the militia rate. This would enable the militia to respond swiftly to emergencies. Some problems remained: for example, the Commons disliked a proposal that the militia should be able to enter property forcibly in daytime. The bill finally passed in May 1662 (**118**).

The summer of 1662 was an anxious time, with the new militia not yet settled and fears of disorder when the Church settlement came into force in August. Five more army regiments were raised in September and in December the lords lieutenant were ordered to levy the £70,000 for that year. In 1663 an Act allowed each militia unit to be kept on foot for up to fourteen days, which meant that part could always be on duty, except during the harvest and the depths of winter. By late 1663 Charles could feel more confident of his ability to deal with disturbances. The new militia was settled under politically reliable officers, with funds provided until the end of 1664. His army – regular regiments and independent companies in garrisons – now amounted to more than 8,000 men. Parliament resisted anything which might imply recognition of a 'standing army' (identified with tyranny), but raised no real objection to the king's keeping up these forces at his own expense as 'guards and garrisons': they were so widely dispersed that they did not seem to threaten Parliament or people. A rough balance had been achieved between the security of the state and the liberty of the subject. Charles did not think his military resources were adequate, but he was still the first English king to have even a small standing army in peacetime (**43**).

The Constitution and the King's Revenue

The Convention had done little to define the king's powers. The bill to confirm the fundamental laws did not pass and in any case was vague as to how much of the legislation of 1640–60 should remain in force. This question was soon resolved. The Act for the Safety and Preservation of His Majesty's Person and Government declared null and void all acts which had not received the royal assent. Thus the fiscal legislation of 1641, the Triennial Act* and the Acts taking away Star Chamber* and High Commission* were to stand, as was that excluding the bishops from the Lords, but the militia ordinance and all subsequent legislation was nullified.

This did not mean that the legislation to which Charles I had assented should be preserved inviolate, as the Convention's bill had proposed. The Act excluding the bishops from the Lords was soon repealed, as was that part of the Act against High Commission which abolished other church courts. In 1662 and 1663 the Lords considered repealing all the legislation of the Long Parliament, re-enacting only such bills as they thought fit. A committee considered how to set up a court as useful to poor litigants as Star Chamber*, while guarding against the abuses of the 1630s. In 1664, at the second attempt, Charles secured the passage of a new Triennial Act* which expressed the hope that the king would call Parliament often – at least every three years – but, unlike that of 1641, established no machinery to make him do so and laid down no minimum length for sessions (**101**).

If the Cavalier Parliament considered repealing some of the Acts of 1641, it was also reluctant to confirm those of the Convention concerning the indemnity, the confirmation of judicial proceedings and the abolition of wardship. In May the Commons considered a bill to grant an indemnity to the king's faithful subjects and to restore estates wrongfully taken from them, which would overturn both the Indemnity Act and many legal judgments of 1642–60. Only when the king told them that his honour was engaged in the confirmation of these Acts did the Commons comply.

In other ways, the Houses enhanced the king's authority. The Act for the preservation of his person declared the Covenant unlawful and denied that the Houses could legislate without the king. It provided for the punishment of anyone accusing the king of trying to bring in Popery or inciting the people to hate the king. Another Act was designed to prevent large-scale petitioning, which had often, in the 1640s, been a pretext for intimidation. Now petitions could be presented by no more than ten persons. Finally, the 1662 Licensing Act stated that only books and pamphlets licensed by a person in authority could be published. Those writing, printing or selling unlicensed works were to be punished (**106**).

The thinking behind these and the new Militia Acts was obvious: the king needed additional powers to repress the subversive forces which had emerged since 1640. On this, the king and the bulk of the ruling elite agreed, but on other matters, notably taxation, their interests diverged. The Cavalier Parliament left intact the fiscal legislation of 1641: it had no intention of allowing Charles II to raise money in ways not approved by Parliament, as his father had done. The Commons were very sensitive about such matters. In June 1661 they resolved to impeach one John Walter for demanding dues from ships on the pretext of a ballast patent, whereupon the patent was speedily withdrawn. They reacted similarly to later patents to set up lighthouses.

On the other hand, they declared themselves willing to 'settle a full, constant and standing revenue ... such as might befit the support of so great and good a prince and might honourably and effectually maintain and uphold his government' (**10**) and to grant a 'plentiful' supply to meet his immediate needs. Their actions proved less generous than their words. The 'immediate supply' consisted of inviting voluntary contributions, which produced £229,000 – not enough either to meet the king's expenses or to pay off his debts. As for the permanent revenue, the secretary to the treasury, Sir Philip Warwick, showed that the king's basic revenues were yielding some £265,000 a year less than the estimated £1,200,000. The Commons accepted this figure, and started a lengthy investigation into the administration of the excise, to see if its yield could be improved.

The Commons' slowness owed much to a sheer lack of fiscal expertise. MPs always suspected corruption and inefficiency in the administration and had no wish to grant more in taxes than they had to: they had expected the disbanding of the New Model to bring a large cut in taxation [**doc. 16**]. Besides, if they granted too much, the king might feel that he did not need to heed their advice on those issues, like religion, where they did not see eye to eye [**doc. 20**].

They were not wholly unco-operative. In November 1661 they resolved to raise an assessment of £1,200,000 over eighteen months 'for the king's present occasions' and on 1 March 1661 they gave a first reading to a bill for a hearth tax*: perhaps significantly, this followed Charles's announcement that he had approved the Prayer Book, as revised by Convocation*. The long investigation into the excise led to an Act of 1663 which in some ways strengthened the hand of the collectors, but also sought to prevent some of their misdeeds. Jurisdiction over the excise was vested in the JPs, thus giving members of the gentry power to prevent extortion and oppression (**42**).

The spring of 1663 saw the most sustained campaign of the reign to subject the king's revenue to parliamentary scrutiny and control. This was part of the campaign to oust Clarendon and his followers. His enemies claimed that he was behind the opposition to the king's religious policy and that that opposition would disappear if the king gave the Commons satisfaction on other matters. Thus factious courtiers promoted investigations into 'mismanagement' in the hope of finding evidence to support their call for the removal of Clarendon and others (many of them Parliamentarians*) admitted into office in 1660. A bill was brought in to ensure that offices went only to loyal subjects, who conformed to the Church of England. On the production of detailed accounts of the king's finances, various committees and sub-committees were set up to look into various branches of the revenue. Following a report suggesting that the yield could be higher, it was resolved on 8 May to bring in a bill 'for fixing the public charges of the kingdom upon some particular branches of the revenue'. The king was asked to make no arrangements for managing the post office until the Commons had investigated the matter and to revoke all leases of crown lands made for too long a time or at too low a rent. It was claimed that the revenue could be increased by £56,000, but some of the proposed increases were decidedly hypothetical. When the Commons at last agreed to vote an immediate supply they voted a subsidy, which was antiquated and inefficient and brought in less than the free gift of 1661 (**10, 42**).

All this might suggest that the once loyal Cavalier House of Commons was now out of control, but that was not so. These investigations reflected a mixture of endemic backbench suspicion of the misuse of power and deliberate mischief-making by court politicians. Confusion reigned: 'I can neither tell you what the House intends or what we at Whitehall wish they would,' wrote Henry Coventry [**doc. 19**].

In fact, all the sound and fury had little lasting effect. The bill to appropriate each branch of the revenue to particular items of expenditure, which would have imposed rigid constraints on the king's finances, did not pass. The attempts to scrutinise the administration of the crown lands and post office came to nothing. On the positive side, Acts were passed which helped to improve the administration of the excise and hearth money and the Commons cannot have foreseen the poor yield of the subsidy. The discrediting of Temple and Bristol temporarily cooled the fires of faction at court which had helped to enflame the Commons. Despite the haggling and niggling, between 1661 and 1663 the Commons had tried to fulfil their promise of a 'full constant and standing revenue', granting the hearth tax (in perpetuity) and trying to increase the yield of the customs and excise. If the increase was less than expected, this was due partly to trade depression and partly to ignorance of the problems involved: it took twenty years' trial and error to produce the much more efficient revenue system of the 1680s.

It was to be a decade before the ordinary revenue reached the magic figure of £1,200,000: thanks partly to Charles's extravagance and partly to the accumulated burden of debt, this still proved insufficient for his needs (**42**). Parliament had, however, agreed that the king should once more 'live of his own' and had granted him a series of revenues to exploit as best he could, rather than a fixed annual sum. At first, this meant that he received much less than the sum which Parliament had judged necessary, but by the end of the reign he was receiving substantially more. As with the militia, Charles was granted less in revenue that he would have liked, but the end result was far from unsatisfactory.

Religion

The Cavalier House of Commons soon made its religious outlook clear by ordering MPs to take communion according to the Anglican rite and resolving to burn the Covenant. The Act for the preservation of the king's person annulled almost all the ecclesiastical legislation of the 1640s: in the end, only the abolition of High Commission* was to stand. With the decision to restore the bishops to the Lords, it was clear that the Commons wished to restore episcopacy in its old form, without the concessions to the Presbyterians set out in the Worcester House Declaration.

In fact, it was restored without any need for fresh legislation. On 25 June 1661 the Commons read a bill 'to supply any defect in the former laws and to provide for an effectual conformity to the liturgy of the Church'. The Commons saw no need to draft a new Prayer Book, because the legislation requiring the use of that of 1559 was still in force. The bill aimed to ensure that only those who used the Prayer Book services should remain in benefices in the established church. It passed the Commons only to stick in the Lords, which clearly owed much to the king's influence. As promised in the Worcester House Declaration, he had called a synod of divines at the Savoy. The Presbyterians were divided and somewhat demoralised while the bishops, encouraged by the Commons' behaviour, became intransigent.

Convocation* also met, as was usual in time of Parliament. Charles had delayed calling it, fearing (rightly) that the increasingly confident and militant Anglicans would predominate, but he clung to the hope that it might agree to concessions to the Presbyterians: the summons to its members did not include the usual provision that nothing was to be agreed contrary to the liturgy or doctrine of the Church of England. Once Convocation met, its mood was clear and Charles tried to warn it against discussing sensitive topics, such as the Church's government and liturgy (**32**).

By the end of the summer the policy of comprehension and conciliation was on the brink of failure. Meanwhile July saw a concerted attempt to secure toleration for Catholics. The Lords resolved to bring in a bill to repeal some of the more severe laws against them, with provisions for priests to register with the secretary of state. The bill did not pass the Lords and would almost certainly have failed in the Commons. Charles strongly supported it and Clarendon did not oppose it openly, but public opinion was against any sort of toleration. Alarms of 'fanatic' plots reinforced the belief of most Anglicans that all Protestant Dissenters were seditious: the Commons were unconvinced by Clarendon's attempt to distinguish between peaceable and seditious Dissenters. This hardening of attitudes made it improbable that Parliament would agree to any indulgence for Catholics, even as part of a general toleration.

When Parliament reconvened in November Charles told the Houses that religion was too hard a matter for him and referred it to them. He also asked Convocation* to review the Prayer Book.

While this revision was under way, the Lords held up the uniformity bill, which may have provoked the Commons to pass a bill effectively negating the Convention's Act confirming ministers in their livings. The new bill would confirm only those who used the Prayer Book and who had been ordained by a bishop. The Lords rejected the bill, thanks mainly to Clarendon who won over seven bishops and, for once, co-operated with Bristol [**doc. 20**]. Having thwarted this attempt to drive Presbyterian clergymen from their parishes, Charles and Clarendon tried to ensure that some of those clergy remained in the Church, by amending the uniformity bill. On

17 March a proviso was offered to the Lords whereby the king could dispense any beneficed minister from wearing the surplice or using the sign of the cross in baptism [**doc. 21**]. These were small concessions to Presbyterian incumbents compared with those in the Worcester House Declaration. Instead of a wide comprehension Charles offered only a little latitude to selected incumbents, but although the Lords accepted the proviso, the Commons rejected it without a division. They also rejected a proposal that those ejected for nonconformity should receive one fifth of the income of their parishes, a concession granted to Anglicans in the 1640s, and insisted that the provisions for uniformity should be extended to non-beneficed lecturers and schoolmasters. Faced with the Commons' intractability, the Lords backed down.

Charles assented to the uniformity bill, but still hoped to mitigate its rigour. Clarendon told the Houses that

> the execution of these sharp laws depends upon the wisdom of the most discerning, generous and merciful prince, who having had more experience of the nature and humour of mankind than any prince living can best distinguish between the tenderness of conscience and pride of conscience (**18**).

Under the terms of the Act, ministers had to declare their conformity or quit their benefices by 24 August 1662. As the deadline approached, rumours of revolt abounded and the king's forces were on continual alert. Late in August Clarendon sent word to some London Presbyterian ministers that the king wished them to petition to be dispensed from strict compliance with the Act, with a strong hint that the petition would be granted. They petitioned, but the privy council rejected their plea after a vigorous speech from the Bishop of London. Again, Clarendon seemed to advocate conciliation, but this time he clearly acted against his own inclinations. He wrote to Ormond

> The very severe execution of the Act of Uniformity which is resolved on may, I fear, add more fuel to the matter that was before combustible enough. But we are in and must proceed with steadiness and so must you [in Ireland] and I wish I were as confident that we shall do so as that you will.

Whether or not he had earlier preferred conciliation, Clarendon was now convinced that the government had no option but to enforce the Act and that there was little danger of a Presbyterian revolt. Indeed, although some 1,800 ministers lost their livings, the exodus was peaceful. If Clarendon publicly supported conciliation, this was because he had to comply with his master's wishes (**64**).

The ambivalence of his position was seen again in Charles's last attempt to weaken the Act of Uniformity. Late in December he issued a declaration stating his dislike of persecution and his hope that Parliament would pass legislation acknowledging his power to dispense with the Act's provisions and to reduce the burdens on Catholics (**16**). This was merely a declaration of intent, which in itself did nothing for Dissenters or Catholics. Mention of the latter reflected the increased activity of the court Catholics, led by Bristol and the queen mother. The hopes expressed in the declaration that Parliament might reverse its stand on religion may seem naive. They can perhaps be explained by Charles's telling the French ambassador that he had 'taken measures' with some peers and MPs and expected them to prove amenable – probably a reference to Bennet and Bristol's new approach to parliamentary management.

Clarendon was in an awkward position. He must have regarded the declaration (especially the references to Catholics) as foolish and provocative, but if he opposed it openly he would lose the king's favour. His gout offered a way out. When Bennet read him a draft of the declaration he raised various objections. When these were met, he said that declarations were a ticklish commodity and the important thing was that it should do no harm. He implied that he was in such pain that he could not concentrate but he was well enough to receive the French ambassador at about this time. When Parliament reconvened in February 1663 he claimed to be too ill to attend.

On 23 February a bill was brought into the Lords to allow the king to dispense individuals from complying with the Act of Uniformity and other laws imposing conformity or oaths in religious matters. It would also empower him to issue licences to peaceable Protestants to worship in their own way. None of these benefits was to apply to Catholics, nor could those holding benefices in the Church of England be dispensed from conforming to its liturgy. Charles had thus finally abandoned any hope of comprehension and was seeking a limited toleration.

The Lords amended the bill to apply only to the Act of Uniformity, thus making doubly sure that it could not benefit the Catholics. The Commons meanwhile resolved to draw up reasons against indulgence to Dissenters and to bring in a bill against the growth of Popery. When Clarendon reappeared in the Lords on 12 March, he moved to adjourn debate on the dispensing bill for a month, which, in effect, shelved it indefinitely. He drew up an answer to the

Commons' reasons on the king's behalf [**doc. 22**], but there is no evidence that it was ever delivered.

In abandoning his attempt to give a statutory basis to his dispensing power, Charles finally accepted the Act of Uniformity. If he wished to help Catholics and Protestant Dissenters, he would have to do so by not enforcing the laws against them. His attitude to Dissenters was ambivalent. Some, he thought, were basically peaceable, but were goaded into revolt by persecution; these deserved a measure of indulgence. Others were irreconcilable and seditious and he oscillated between a policy of repression (to hold them down) and toleration (to propitiate them). They seemed most dangerous during the wars with the Dutch, in which they might act as a Calvinist fifth column. In 1665, at the start of the Second Dutch War, a repressive policy was used, with the Five Mile Act, designed to drive Dissenting ministers away from their congregations and from towns. With the Third Dutch War, in 1672 the king switched to the second policy, with the Declaration of Indulgence.

The Restoration Church settlement was a humiliating defeat for the king. Both personal preference and political calculation inclined him to favour comprehension and toleration. The Cavalier House of Commons (and the bulk of the ruling elite) was irreconcilably hostile to both Dissent and Popery. The gentry did much more than the clergy to shape the religious settlement. They drafted and passed legislation and took the lead in harassing and ejecting non-Anglican ministers and persecuting Dissenting congregations. The Anglican clergy, by contrast, were initially uncertain of their position and slow to gain confidence The gentry's role was symbolised by the eventual passage of a bill to restore advowsons* and impropriated tithes* confiscated from laymen in the 1640s. Lay domination over the Church, briefly interrupted, was restored.

This in itself was indicative of a fundamental feature of the Restoration settlement. If the king was granted extensive powers, this was not because he was in a position to demand such powers, but because the ruling elite, as represented in Parliament, *wanted* him to have them. Scared by the upheavals of 1640–60, they believed that effective monarchy was necessary to maintain order, hierarchy and subordination. However, they expected the king to use those powers in a manner compatible with their interests and prejudices. How far those expectations would be met remained to be seen.

Part Two: The Reign of Charles II

4 Society and Government

The Restoration brought a reinforcement of the social order which existed before the civil war, in which wealth was very unequally distributed and the wealthy few ruled the many. Despite the growth of some types of trade, notably with the colonies, the economy remained mainly agricultural. London's population was about half a million, but the next largest town, Norwich, had little more than 20,000 inhabitants. The great majority of England's five million or so people lived in villages or small market towns. Poor transport made the carriage of bulky goods expensive and encouraged a large measure of local self-sufficiency. While London and larger provincial towns boasted a high level of literacy and of knowledge of the outside world, many small towns and villages were preoccupied by local matters, their information on politics supplied by out-of-date newsletters and the official *Gazette*. The ferment of political debate in the 1640s had created a hunger for information – foreigners remarked on the knowledge and boldness with which Londoners discussed politics – but the reimposition of censorship meant that that hunger could not be fully satisfied.

For the illiterate, the majority in rural areas and a large minority in towns, censorship made little difference. Most plodded through the farming year with little awareness of events at national level. For such people, little affected by religious or political radicalism, the Restoration must have made little difference, except that they could once more celebrate Christmas and other Christian festivals and were less likely to be maltreated by soldiers.

The bulk of the landed elite, Parliamentarians as well as Royalists, had been badly shaken by the events of the late 1640s and 1650s. The traditional social order seemed to be toppling, with base-born army officers ordering around members of long-established county families. The alarm which the old elite felt helps to explain the vindictiveness shown at the Restoration and Parliament's concern to build up the king's power, to ensure that such upheavals would not happen again.

Both personal inclination and political commonsense led Charles to accept that the landed elite should resume its direction of local government. Unlike Louis XIV, he had almost no professional officials in the provinces until the development of the excise administration in the 1680s. Traditionally the Crown relied on the leading men of the counties, who possessed the local standing needed to command respect and also, it was hoped, the education and personal qualities to discharge their responsibilities diligently. The English system of local government, centred on the JPs*, involved an alliance of interests between Crown and gentry from which both derived advantages. The gentry enhanced their local prestige and gained the power to regulate the affairs of the locality and punish the misdeeds of the lower orders. The Crown had local government carried on and provided rewards for men of political weight at no financial cost.

It was a system of local government that grew so naturally out of England's social and institutional order that its revival at the Restoration must have seemed inevitable. Local defence was again entrusted to the militia, itself a microcosm of county society, with gentlemen officers commanding artisans and countrymen. With land, the main source of wealth, concentrated in a few hands, such a system seemed natural. Only the gentry·possessed the economic power as landlords and employers, the inherited status (and the deference that went with it) and the education and leisure which together gave them almost a prescriptive right to rule their counties and enter Parliament.

In much the same way, town government usually remained the preserve of the richest inhabitants, who alone could support the often considerable expense of municipal office and did not need to devote all their time to a business or profession. Even in villages, the offices of constable, churchwarden and overseer of the poor were usually held by the more substantial villagers. At every level there was a considerable measure of self-government, although the circle of those who participated was usually narrow. As the king's apparatus of government and powers of coercion were weak – his standing army was small and widely dispersed – he depended heavily on the responsibility and probity of those involved in local government.

How well local governors lived up to their responsibilities varied. Parish officials were variously accused of laxity and petty tyranny. The rulers of towns showed an increasing tendency towards oligarchy and were often accused of using their position for their own profit, misusing corporation property and dining lavishly at the town's expense. Gentlemen, too, often behaved arbitrarily or selfishly. Many early Stuart landlords pushed rents up as high as the market would bear, evicted those who could not pay and tried to establish proprietorial rights over common land. Some used their power as JPs to harass the victims of such practices or turned a blind eye to the chicanery and strong-arm tactics of fellow-landowners.

On the other hand, Tudor and early Stuart governments tried to enforce a wide range of regulations designed to protect the poor against undue exploitation, notably by trying to maintain adequate supplies of grain at moderate prices. Where such preventive measures proved insufficient, the poor laws provided that those unable to work should receive money to buy food and the able-bodied unemployed should be set to work.

The cynical might argue that such measures reflected a simple fear of disorder. With the population rising, too many people were chasing too little food and too little work. Prices (especially food prices) rose, unemployment and underemployment grew, real wages fell. Sheer hunger might drive people to riot, as contemporaries were well aware. Fear of disorder underlay some measures, such as the severe treatment of vagrants, but behind others there was a concern for justice and even a certain compassion, as shown by the severity against grain speculators, the concern for the old, the sick and children, and the many bequests to the poor. The self-interest of the ruling elite might find expression not in the maximisation of rents but in seeking to stand well in the eyes of the poor. Compared with most continental aristocracies, the conduct of the Tudor and early Stuart gentry seems in many ways responsible and just (**92**).

After 1660 the most striking change in the working of local government is a decline in central government interference and direction. Elizabethan and early Stuart governments bombarded JPs with directives, culminating in the Book of Orders of 1630–1, which prescribed rigidly and in detail the laws the JPs should enforce and how they should enforce them. The distrust which this implied created ill-feeling, but there was to be no such problem under Charles II. The king and privy council expected JPs to ensure that the royal revenue was collected. In times of political tension JPs were ordered to search the homes of suspicious persons or to enforce the laws against Dissenters or Catholics.

On more routine matters, however, such as social and economic regulation, highways and bridges, JPs were left to their own devices. This led to a growing diversity of administrative practice, as authorities in counties and towns reacted to new problems in different ways. In many towns, householders had long been responsible for cleansing, repairing and lighting the streets outside their homes, while highways and bridges were to be maintained by the parishes in which they stood. With urban growth and the increase in wheeled traffic, such a diffusion of responsibility allowed the roads to deteriorate, so these tasks were transferred either to *ad hoc* bodies of paving or cleansing commissioners, or to the corporation or county as a whole. The responsibilities of the individual or parish were commuted into a money rate. The speed at which this process occurred, and the forms it took, varied greatly, but the outcome was that the organs of local government became more numerous and various in the century after 1660 (**53, 60, 61**).

Leaving JPs to their own devices also led to changes in the direction of social and economic policy, which were reflected in parliamentary legislation. Even before 1660 central government was showing less interest in regulating the grain market, perhaps because the methods used proved ineffective, perhaps because the poor law offered another means of providing for the poor, perhaps because grain prices were levelling off and even starting to fall. The population rise had virtually stopped by the 1650s, prices were stabilising and real wages beginning to rise. Dearth and poverty did not disappear: there were famine prices in some areas in 1661–2, 1678–9 and above all 1709–10. Unemployment and underemployment remained endemic: many unskilled workers found work only intermittently and at low wages. In 1696 Gregory King calculated that about half the population 'decreased the wealth of the kingdom', or consumed more than they produced. Central government, however, now showed little interest in the preventive, or palliative, measures so often ordered earlier in the century. Some JPs still tried to enforce the old regulations on grain marketing and against speculation, especially in years of dearth, when failure to take even cosmetic action could provoke riots.

In general, however, these regulations fell increasingly into disuse. The landed elite thus ceased to protect the consumer, while at the same time trying to help the producer, reversing the earlier order of priorities. Grain imports were restricted, unless prices at home rose to near-famine levels. From 1673 there were various provisions for bounties on grain exports, the aim being to siphon off England's surplus production and so prevent prices falling too far in years of relative abundance. Similarly, the Act of 1666 against importing Irish cattle was intended to keep up the price of English beasts. Together with the game laws, such legislation could be seen as evidence that the landed elite became more self-centred after 1660. Economic conditions were turning against landowners: farm prices were levelling off, profits and rents were falling.

Was the landed elite using its political power to shore up its economic position at the expense of the poor? It should first be mentioned that it is uncertain how far corn bounties and the like affected price levels (although England was unusual in not experiencing a fall in prices after 1650) and that real wages (admittedly a statistical abstraction) rose substantially in the century after 1650. The poor relief system now raised and paid out far more than in the first half of the century. The Act of Settlement of 1662 tried to restrict eligibility for relief in any parish to those 'settled' there: newcomers and squatters could be made to move on. It seems, however, that newcomers were often treated more harshly by parish officials than by JPs, who were often flexible and sympathetic (**109**).

In general, the image of ruthlessly selfish landowners, oppressing all below them, seems something of a caricature. Economic circumstances militated against such behaviour. As farming became less profitable and rents fell, efficient tenants could dictate terms to landlords. Many landlords found it wiser to write off rent arrears in bad years than to have no tenants. The increased importance of electoral politics made it advisable for a politically ambitious landlord to maintain his tenants' goodwill: he might need their votes (**96, 123**).

When one considers wider aspects of fiscal and economic policy, the idea that the landed elite was obsessively selfish becomes even harder to sustain. True, the abolition of wardship* removed an occasional and irritating burden on those who held land by certain feudal tenures, while the king was compensated at the expense of the consumer. It is also true that the Commons imposed no *permanent* tax on land and, in temporary grants, often placed the burden on trade or consumption rather than land. However, when it was necessary to raise a large sum quickly they relied on monthly assessments, which fell mainly on land. They reverted to the old subsidy in 1663, because unlike the assessment it was based on net rather than gross income, and so allowed for the deduction of 'necessary' expenses. It brought in so little that the Commons never used it again, but in 1671 they considered how to convert it into a 'new subsidy', which would fall only on net income but produce a large and predictable yield.

Thus the Commons did not single-mindedly shift the burden of taxation away from land. Moreover, when voting taxes on trade they showed considerable discrimination. New customs duties were designed to boost exports and inhibit imports, especially those from

France. A similar concern for the promotion of trade was seen in the Navigation Acts of the early 1660s which renewed and extended that of 1651. These were intended to protect England's expanding colonial trades against Dutch and other interlopers and to ensure that English shippers carried a higher proportion of the goods brought into English ports.

Such an approach to fiscal and economic matters does not suggest that the predominantly landed Parliament was concerned exclusively with the interests of landowners; many MPs had a wider conception of their responsibilities. On the other hand, because of the wealth and power of the landed elite, Charles had to retain its trust and goodwill, in local government and in Parliament. The next chapter will, therefore, deal with national politics.

5   Politics and the Constitution

The Restoration settlement showed the concern of the ruling elite (as represented in Parliament) to re-establish what they saw as the traditional balance of the constitution. The king should possess the powers needed to run the government. He should choose his own advisers and officials. He was responsible for the formulation of policy, at home and abroad. He should protect his subjects against revolt and invasion, maintain law and order and dispense justice. He should defend the established church, suppress heresy and schism and promote Christian morality. All these powers were, or should have been, used for the subject's benefit, to help create a secure, ordered society, permeated by Christian values and the rule of law. At the same time, the subject should be protected by the laws against possible abuses of royal power, especially arbitrary interference with property or personal liberty: English kings could not make laws or levy taxes without consent.

Kept within these limits, monarchy seemed not a colourful anachronism but the most rational, effective and beneficial form of government. Democracy, it was widely believed, degenerated into anarchy, aristocracy slid into oligarchy, unlimited monarchy soon became tyranny, but limited monarchy combined the best features of each without the vices, reconciling order and liberty. Thus the king needed to be strong enough to fulfil his responsibilities to his people, but not strong enough to oppress them. The constraints on him were, however, more moral and political than legal or constitutional. A king with limited powers of coercion, who depended so much on the voluntary co-operation of his subjects, would be wise not to antagonise them too much or too often.

However, as Charles I had shown, if a king was determined to stretch his powers to the limit, neither the law courts nor Parliament could stop him. Before 1641 the king could raise money without Parliament in so many ways that, if Parliament denied him money with a view to extracting concessions, he raised it elsewhere. Experience of Charles I's misgovernment forced the Long Parliament to tamper with the traditional constitutional balance, to restrict the king's use of powers which his predecessors had been trusted to exercise at will. These restrictions went against most MPs' constitutional instincts and stemmed not from a desire for change but from a concern for self-preservation.

By 1660 the position had changed. Charles I was dead and in most respects the Parliamentarians' quarrel had been with him, not with the monarchy. His son could reasonably be given the benefit of the doubt. Meanwhile, the upheavals since 1640 made an effective monarchy doubly necessary. To restore the traditional balance, an added emphasis needed to be put on the king's authority. Aspects which had been taken for granted were forcefully and explicitly restated, because they had recently been challenged. Acts were passed stating that the king alone should direct the militia and that the two Houses could not legislate without him. Fearful of the danger from radicals and republicans, speakers in positions of authority went out of their way to stress the divine attributes of kingship. Kings, they argued, derived their power from God, not from the people. If they abused that power, their subjects should not resist but suffer passively, leaving it to God to punish their monarch's misdeeds (**57**) [**doc. 23**].

Such arguments were intended to counter others, advanced during the civil wars, that subjects could resist the king when it was a matter of self-preservation and that England's government was (or should be) essentially popular – indeed, that sovereignty originated with the people. Conservative writers after 1660 clearly feared that such arguments could undermine loyalty to the restored regime and many historians claim that the ideas developed in 1640–60 fatally weakened the monarchy's ideological foundations (**119**).

But did they? Historians living in a parliamentary democracy are likely to find the ideas of Parliamentarians and Levellers more familiar and congenial than those of the proponents of divine-right monarchy. It is far from clear that those who mattered politically in Charles II's England felt the same way. The reimposition of censorship and the government's tampering with the mails inhibited the expression of unorthodox political views, but it still seems that, however much they have fascinated historians, the ideas of the Levellers and their like won only limited support in their own day. The ruling elite seems largely to have accepted that hierarchy and authority in state and society were interdependent: divine-right monarchy and an aristocratic social order went naturally together.

Restoration Englishmen were not faced with a stark choice between royal absolutism and popular sovereignty. The tradition of responsible monarchy, of a balance between the king's power and the subject's rights, offered a middle way which was widely acceptable. It was quite possible, within the context of that tradition, to criticise abuses of royal power without undermining the king's authority or suggesting that it originated in the people's consent (**49**). In the words of Sir Orlando Bridgeman

> Though this is an absolute monarchy, yet this is so far from infringing the people's rights that the people, as to their properties, liberties and lives, have as great a privilege as the king. It is not the sharing of government that is for the liberty and benefit of the people; but it is how far they may have their lives and liberties and estates safely secured under government.

In the 1640s there had been a ferment of discussion about the origins and nature of government. For much of Charles II's reign there was very little. There were frequent arguments about the way the king used his authority in particular cases, but the foundations and legitimacy of that authority were rarely questioned. This was partly because the restored monarchy was so generally accepted, partly because to discuss the origins of government revived unpleasant memories of the civil wars. Even when the Exclusion Crisis raised such issues, by implication, the Exclusionist Whigs (in Parliament at least) tried hard to avoid discussing them. Only in the debates about the change of ruler in 1689 did the Whigs lose their inhibitions (**37, 86, 88**).

While it may seem to historians that the new political ideas of 1640–60 ought to have weakened the restored monarchy, there is little hard evidence that they did so. If anything, the reverse seems likely. Having seen the upheaval which accompanied such ideas, the ruling elite was determined to deny them expression and ignore them, except perhaps for the purposes of attacking them. The reaction against the world's being turned upside down explains the re-establishment of monarchy on traditional lines, with a large, independent revenue; but (as we have seen) Parliament would not trust Charles too far or give him the means to abuse his authority. Its members wanted him to rule as his predecessors should have ruled – wisely, responsibly and in the best interests of his people in general and the landed elite in particular.

The Restoration settlement reflected an ideal of constitutional balance and a body of political expectations which together defined the framework within which Charles was to govern. If he remained within the limits of that framework he would be able to enjoy considerable discretion and exercise substantial power, with little fear of controversy or disorder. If he overstepped those limits, if he seemed to threaten the constitutional balance, if he wilfully ignored those political expectations, there was likely to be trouble. Everything depended on Charles's skills as king and politician and his willingness to confine himself to the politically feasible.

At this point, one should remember the advantages and disadvantages of hindsight. A historian can use contemporary diaries and letters and the reports of foreign ambassadors to build up a broadly-based impression of opinion within the ruling elite and in Parliament. Much of this information was not available to Charles II. Just as one ruler could not see another's secret diplomatic dispatches and had to deduce his intentions from his actions, so Charles could not see inside his subjects' hearts and minds. He attended some debates in the Lords, but none in the Commons, and relied on second-hand accounts of their supposedly secret proceedings. Whereas now, with a well-established tradition of mass politics, the media offer copious information on political events and attitudes, under Charles II the press was censored and politicians felt less need to publicise their views or to justify their conduct to a wider public. Charles's information on politics was, therefore, deficient.

Moreover, just as in diplomacy a ruler's interpretation of another's actions was often distorted by misguided preconceptions about the other's character and intentions, so Charles's understanding of politics was distorted by misconceptions about his subjects. He had been twelve in 1642. He had grown up amid the turmoil of civil war and the uncertainty of exile. In trying to explain his father's execution he looked back beyond Pride's Purge and the rise of the New Model to the civil war itself. Although most Parliamentarians had not wished to abolish the monarchy or to kill the king, one could with hindsight see their making war on him as leading inexorably to his execution. It would also seem logical that the roots of regicide should lie in a disaffection far more widespread than that of the few army officers and Rumpers who brought it about.

Thus, while the historian can argue that all but a handful of Charles II's subjects were loyal to the monarchy, one can understand why Charles should have believed otherwise. His distrust was reinforced by the sometimes ill-tempered disputes and criticism in Parliament, which he (and others) were all too ready to explain in terms of republicanism and disaffection, reviving memories of 1640–2 [**doc. 19**].

There have been numerous claims that Charles inclined towards 'absolutism'*. Louis XIV's regime certainly seemed a model of efficiency. The concentration in the king of authority and decision-making facilitated the more effective mobilisation of France's resources for war and so helped make her the greatest power in Europe. To many France's government seemed more progressive and rational than England's (with the awkward division of revenue-raising and legislative powers between Crown and Parliament) or the antique federalism of the Dutch Republic.

Charles was impressed by Louis XIV's regime and in an ideal world might have liked to imitate it: he was always, to Clarendon's disgust, attracted by novelty. There is, however, little evidence that he seriously intended to make England's government like that of France. Absolutism was a specifically French form of government, which had developed as kings and officials struggled to overcome problems which were in many ways different from those of England. France had a far more complex and cumbersome administration, with great variations between the provinces, which made it very difficult to establish effective control over the provinces and to use their wealth and manpower in war. In order to overcome the vast tangle of local and corporate vested interests, royal officials developed harsh, authoritarian methods, which they justified by means of an authoritarian political and legal theory.

French absolutism developed from the need to tackle huge administrative and fiscal problems. Tough methods were needed to wear down the intermediate authorities (provinces, towns, seigneurs) which stood between the Crown and its subjects and to overcome Frenchmen's reluctance to pay taxes. The French kings did not develop these methods in pursuit of any theory or model of government, but were driven to act in this way by pressing practical needs. France was partially surrounded by the territories of the French kings' inveterate rivals, the Habsburgs. This 'encirclement' created a constant threat of war and forced the Crown to raise all the men and money it could from its diverse and recalcitrant territories. Its efforts were eagerly abetted by officials whose power and profits were enhanced by the extension of royal authority.

By contrast, the problems and the apparatus of government of the English kings were smaller. England's island position allowed them, to a large extent, to opt out of European politics if they chose. The Crown's military commitments were small – defending the Scots border and maintaining English rule in Ireland – and the former was no longer necessary under Charles II. It did not need a standing army or (thanks to the tradition of local self-government) a large bureaucracy. Institutionally, England was much more integrated than France. Governed as a nation for centuries, it had a single system of law and local government and a single national representative institution, whereas France still possessed some provincial representative bodies, or estates, while the national Estates General met rarely and achieved little.

Stuart Englishmen saw in Parliament the embodiment of the difference between the English and French constitutions. Over the centuries, English kings had found that it was easier to get taxes paid and laws obeyed if they first sought the consent of their leading subjects. This reliance on, and need for, consent was a product of the kings' weak means of coercion, but also served to perpetuate that weakness. Where French kings relied on authority and force, the English sought consent and co-operation at every level, from Parliament to parish. This seemed to foreign observers a feeble and inefficient form of government, but it worked quite well, partly because of the responsibility and public spirit of much of the ruling elite, partly because the Crown's demands were usually small. A large bureaucracy and standing army made for a high level of taxation, with troops and officials needed to collect it. The English Crown found it hard to raise enough money to fight a major war, but after 1689 it became clear that even that was possible, if Parliament was committed to it.

Given the institutional differences between the two countries, it would have been unrealistic and irrelevant to consider establishing 'absolutism' in England. Louis XIV's success owed much to the fact that the ruling elite and the king's officials generally accepted the principles of absolutism. There was no such acceptance in England. Charles II's officials were careful to keep within the law and few, if any, of the ruling elite would have accepted that he could tax or legislate without consent.

On the other hand, Louis XIV was able to exact obedience largely because he kept within certain political limits. He respected the privileges of the nobility and the vested interests of his officials and treated his subjects more fairly than his predecessors had done. Here he had much in common with Charles II. Successful kingship depended not on trying to imitate some theoretical model of government but on making the best use of existing institutions, within limits set by the need to retain the support of the 'political nation'.

Thus for Charles II, had he appreciated it, the problem was to exploit the surge of feeling in favour of monarchy after the civil wars, so as to build up his revenues and maintain peace and order at home. Parliament might vote more revenue if it judged that such revenue was required for good government, it might marginally strengthen his means of coercion if it feared disorder, but the Crown's powers could be increased only with the support of a substantial part of the ruling elite. As one of Charles's ministers wrote: 'Till the king can fall into the humour of his people, he can never be great'(**40, 49, 91**) [**doc. 24**].

For the king to build upon his subjects' support required mutual trust, but Charles was not disposed to trust his subjects. Bitter experience had left him wary and cynical. Fear of rebellion led him to practise a mixture of repression and conciliation. Had he felt strong enough, he would probably have crushed the Dissenters. As he did not, he tried to propitiate them, by giving offices to Presbyterians in 1660 and by promoting comprehension and toleration. It is likely, too, that insecurity influenced his foreign policy. His fondness for France and hostility to the Dutch perhaps owed something to commercial considerations, although by the 1670s the French too had emerged as a serious economic threat. Charles also probably preferred, on principle, France's monarchy to Dutch republicanism and wanted revenge for the destruction of much of his fleet in the Medway in 1667. Above all, however, Louis had a large army and, until 1673, the Dutch did not. For a king who feared revolt, to have such a powerful ally was reassuring.

Charles's insecurity thus led him, at times, to conciliate the Dissenters and reinforced his liking for France. Such policies created a distrust of his intentions which was to force him to dissolve the Cavalier Parliament in 1679, but they were not the only cause of his difficulties with Parliament. His distrust of his subjects extended to politicians. He believed his ministers pursued their own interests, rather than his. Had he been prepared to put in the necessary effort, he might have controlled them by checking on their recommendations. As he could not be bothered to do so, he tried to balance individuals and factions, so that nobody gained a monopoly of favour.

Thus in 1662-3 he continued to place considerable trust in Clarendon despite his favour to Bennet and Bristol, while in his last years he kept Halifax in office although he was at odds with his fellow-ministers. Such rule by faction could work if the factions' rivalry was kept within limits of discipline and decorum. No such limits existed at Charles II's court, which was frivolous, promiscuous and chaotically informal. Charles was as ready to receive political advice from personal servants as from senior ministers, especially if they made it amusing. He did little to stop courtiers carrying their feuds into Parliament and seems not to have understood the possible dangers of their doing so [**docs. 25, 26, 27**].

The parliamentary history of the reign divides into two distinct phases, with a watershed around 1672. Before then, court faction did much to sour and unsettle the king's relationship with the Commons. Bristol and Bennet's efforts to undermine Clarendon disrupted the session of 1663. With the loss of the fleet in the Medway in 1667 Clarendon's enemies saw a new chance to unseat him. They were led by Bennet, now Earl of Arlington, and the second Duke of Buckingham, whose ability to amuse the king was exceeded only by his lack of political principle and direction. They convinced Charles that the only way to prevent a major crisis when Parliament met was to dismiss Clarendon. When Charles did so, they went further and argued that only Clarendon's death would satisfy the Commons.

The king was persuaded. While the Commons showed only a limited interest in Clarendon's impeachment, Charles canvassed the Lords, urging them to condemn his most loyal servant. Rarely does one see so clearly the self-centred ruthlessness behind Charles's affable façade: to save his skin, he would sacrifice anyone, no matter how innocent.

When Clarendon fled into exile, Arlington and Buckingham turned on his followers. Supported by ambitious MPs kept out of office by Clarendon, they encouraged the Commons to investigate the mismanagement of the Dutch War, hoping to drive out of office those in the financial and naval administration who were protégés of Clarendon and his son-in-law, the Duke of York (who was lord admiral). So long as they purported to be seeking out maladministration. Clarendon's enemies had much backbench support. They also, however, revived the idea of making the Church more comprehensive and of granting toleration to Dissenters, mainly because most of Clarendon's followers were committed Anglicans. Arlington and Buckingham convinced Charles that the Dissenters were more numerous and powerful than the Anglicans and that the Commons would now agree to changes in the Church.

The Commons reacted to the investigation into misgovernment and to the attempts to weaken the Church in very different ways, but each caused rancour and turmoil. The average backbencher, always ready to suspect corruption and incompetence in high places, eagerly supported the investigation. He was also, however, firmly committed to the Church of England, and the Commons responded to the proposals in favour of Dissent with new bills against conventicles*.

Suddenly, early in 1670, Charles dropped his support for concessions to the Dissenters. The Commons, delighted, voted extra duties on wines for eight years. They lost enthusiasm for the investigation into mismanagement after Charles told them they he could find no evidence that anything was amiss. Soon afterward, he assented to a conventicle bill [**doc. 28**]. After the storms of the past two or three years the sessions of 1670–1 were harmonious and constructive, which showed that if the king gave the Commons the policies they wanted, they would respond positively and even generously (**25**). Despite Charles's politically perverse determination to favour Dissent, despite the immorality, corruption and factionalism of his court, the Commons were still ready to believe in the basic integrity of his government. They might haggle about how much money to grant and how to raise it, but usually voted something in the end. They might dislike some of his policies, some aspects of his style of government, but saw no reason to doubt that he would maintain the constitutional balance re-established at the Restoration.

After 1672, this was no longer so. The composition and basic attitudes of the Commons had hardly changed, but developments at court shattered beyond recall the trust which underlay the relations of Crown and Parliament in the 1660s. The rest of the reign was to be unsettled by fears that the king and his advisers wished to establish 'Popery and arbitrary government' [**doc. 29**].

In 1667 the Dutch made peace with Charles because they feared French expansion into the Spanish Netherlands – roughly present-day Belgium – which acted as a buffer-zone between France and the Dutch Republic. In 1668 the Dutch, England and Sweden signed the Triple Alliance, intended to stop France expanding to the north. No sooner had Charles signed it than he began to seek a closer liaison with France. His duplicity and his refusal to confide fully in any of his advisers make it impossible to be certain about his motives. It may be that the turbulent sessions of 1668–9 made him fearful of rebellion, and so in need of a strong ally, but such a need must have seemed less pressing by the time he signed the Secret Treaty of Dover in May 1670, in which he agreed to join with France in attacking the Dutch and to declare himself a Catholic. In return, Louis would pay him a subsidy and provide military aid if his conversion provoked disorder.

It is difficult to find a convincing explanation for Charles's promise to announce his conversion, but it is unlikely that he was sincere. In a sense, his motives are unimportant, as the promise remained secret and he showed no sign of acting on it. Of much more immediate political importance was the Anglo-French attack on the Dutch in 1672. Many Englishmen saw Louis as an aggressive proponent of Popery and absolutism who wished to dominate Western Europe: once he had overrun the Spanish Netherlands and Dutch Republic, he would turn on England. His demand for freedom of worship for Dutch Catholics gave a religious dimension to the war and it seemed ominous that Charles was taking the 'Catholic' side.

Such anxieties were compounded by Charles's Declaration of Indulgence of March 1672, in which he claimed that his ecclesiastical prerogatives entitled him to suspend the laws against Dissenters, license them to open meeting houses and allow Catholics to worship freely in their homes. This declaration went some way to earning the money which Louis had paid for Charles's conversion and was intended to reduce the danger of the Dissenters making trouble during the war. It provoked alarm for several reasons. The claim that the king could suspend religious statutes might be extended into a claim to suspend any law. Some resented the liberty granted to Dissenters, others the concessions to Catholics. It was even alleged that, as Catholics did not need licences, they were granted a greater freedom than Dissenters (**89, 90**).

A third development at this time was a growing awareness that the Duke of York had become a Catholic. Despite his many bastards, Charles had no legitimate children, so York was still his heir-presumptive. When he failed to take communion at Easter and Christmas 1672 tongues began to wag. The prospect of a Catholic king was alarming. English Protestants saw Catholicism as both theologically wrong and a malign political force. Papists were thought to be forever plotting against Protestant rulers, urged on by priests eager for temporal power and popes seeking universal dominion. Once in power they would not rest until, with implacable cruelty, they had rooted out Protestantism. James's conversion seemed doubly threatening in the light of other developments. The Indulgence showed undue favour to Papists and sought to extend the royal prerogative. And why should Charles choose this time to join with the champion of Popery and absolutism to attack a Protestant state? Everything seemed to point to a design to bring in 'Popery and arbitrary government', involving James, and perhaps Charles as well. Once the Dutch had been defeated, the French army would be free to help in this design: some British regiments were already in the French service. The war also provided a pretext to raise an army at home. Many people – even the soldiers themselves – expressed anxiety about the use to which this army might be put [**doc. 30**].

A deep distrust thus underlay the Commons' aggressive and even hysterical behaviour in 1673. They agreed to give money for the war, but delayed passing the necessary bill until Charles withdrew the Declaration of Indulgence. Later, their refusal to vote any more money forced Charles to make peace with the Dutch early in 1674. When York married an Italian Catholic (his first wife having died) the Commons demanded that the marriage should not be consummated, an unprecedented interference in the private life of a member of the royal family. (York had two daughters, both Protestants, by his first wife. If he now had a son, who would take precedence over them in the succession, he would presumably be brought up as a Catholic, which raised the prospect of a succession of Catholic kings, even if Charles outlived James.) The court was rent with panic and recriminations; politicians sought to divert the Commons' anger on to their colleagues [**doc. 27**]. There were suggestions that York should be sent away from court or disinherited. Charles, usually so cocksure and cynical, consulted an astrologer about the most propitious time to call Parliament.

In time the panic passed. The war ended, the new army units were disbanded. Charles found a new adviser, the Earl of Danby, who tried to increase the royal revenue and to give the Commons the policies they wanted [**doc. 31**]. That, however, proved difficult. Charles was reluctant to abandon the French, and James was still a Catholic, so a residue of distrust remained which undermined Danby's strategy of appealing to MPs' Anglicanism and conservatism. When, in 1678, Charles finally agreed to join with the Dutch against France, many claimed that this was merely a pretext to raise an army. Doubts were expressed about the court's intentions, like those of 1673.

Tension was already high when Titus Oates came along with a story of a Popish Plot to murder the king. This brought the problem of the 'Popish successor' into the open. From the spring of 1679 to the spring of 1681 the central issue in politics was whether James, as a Catholic, should be excluded from the succession to the throne. The supporters of exclusion (soon called Whigs) argued that his religion would inevitably lead him to impose Popery and absolutism by force. Their opponents, the Tories, argued that it was unjust to condemn James untried and that the Whigs' real aim was to start another civil war and overthrow Church and monarchy. While the Whigs denounced the Tories as 'Papists' and 'favourers of Popery', the Tories alleged that the Whigs were scheming republicans who were not really concerned about Popery at all (**90**) [**doc. 32**].

The polarisation of Whig and Tory grew out of the contest over exclusion. James could be excluded from the crown only by an Act of Parliament, which needed the consent of king, Lords and Commons. In all three general elections of 1679–81 the Exclusionists secured a majority in the Commons, but the king and Lords remained opposed to exclusion. Deadlock ensued, comparable with that in 1641–2 over Strafford's attainder or the militia bill. As in 1641–2, the Commons' leaders tried to put pressure on the Lords and king by mobilising support outside Parliament, through propaganda, petitions and demonstrations. Claiming that James planned a military coup, they demanded the removal of his 'creatures' from the armed forces, thus challenging the king's control of the militia and army. As the Anglican clergy, encouraged by James's promises to stand by the Church, rallied to his defence, the Whigs denounced them as favourers of Popery and demanded toleration for Dissenters, in order to unite all Protestants against the Popish menace. Thus in several ways the Whigs' conduct raised echoes of the early 1640s.

The Tories took their stand on the defence of 'Church and king'. Again, the political, ecclesiastical and social order seemed to be threatened from below, so the Tories insisted that the existing order was divinely ordained and that resistance to authority was against the law of God. Such arguments came naturally to members of the ruling elite and of a hierarchically ordered Church. In essence they were those of the old Cavaliers in the early 1660s and drew upon a tradition of emphasis on obedience going back to Tudor times and beyond.

Some Tories perhaps went further than their predecessors in magnifying royal authority. 'All the liberties and privileges the people can pretend to,' wrote Robert Brady, 'were the grants and concessions of the kings of this nation and derived from the crown' (**99**). This implied that the safeguards provided by the law for liberty and property were revocable at the king's pleasure, but the absolutist implications of such arguments were rarely developed and many Tories did not share them (**49, 50**) [**doc. 33**].

The development of such views in the early 1680s does, however, demonstrate the fears of upheaval which the Whigs' conduct aroused. As in the early 1660s the conservative forces in society looked to the Crown to defend the established order and magnified its powers, stressing the impiety of resistance to royal authority.

If the Tories placed more stress on the king's authority than on the subjects' rights, the Whigs tipped the balance the other way.

They emphasised the king's obligation to do what was best for his people and implied that kings existed primarily for their subjects' good. Taken to its logical conclusion this would suggest that the king should agree to whatever his people (as represented in the Commons) thought best, which would reduce his role to that of a figurehead.

Such arguments could be given logical coherence only by arguing that the Commons derived their authority from their representing the sovereign people, but this most Whigs refused to do. As aristocratic as the Tories, the Whig leaders believed that the landed elite should rule. Moreover, arguments for popular sovereignty were associated with the upheavals of 1640–60, which few Whig leaders were prepared to justify. The Whigs were therefore reduced to claiming that although, constitutionally, the king was free to make up his own mind, he had a moral obligation to satisfy his subjects by agreeing to exclusion. Meanwhile, they put pressure on him to agree, relying mainly on exploiting the popular fear of Popery so as to create the impression that a major revolt might ensue if exclusion were not granted (**37, 90**) [**doc. 34**].

In the Exclusion Crisis the Tories claimed monotonously that "41 is here again'. In the sense that it meant a renewed polarisation of the political nation, they were right. The political arguments and electoral mud-slinging created lasting bitterness. In other ways, the similarities with 1640–2 were superficial. Civil war was unlikely, partly because memories of the 1640s acted as a deterrent, partly because the fears exploited by the Whigs were less intense. In order to scare the king into agreeing to exclusion, they exaggerated the scale and commitment of their popular support. It was one thing to vote for candidates who supported exclusion, but quite another to rebel in order to achieve it.

The fears men felt in 1680–1 were far less immediate than those of 1640–2. People were concerned about how the king's possible successor might behave, if he became king. By contrast, people took to the streets in 1641–2 because they feared that the king's soldiers might slaughter them or the cannon in the Tower reduce their houses to rubble. This lower level of immediacy in the Exclusion Crisis helps explain the almost total lack of violence until the last months of 1681, when the Whig cause was already lost (**90**).

Given his fear of rebellion, it was natural that Charles should see the Whigs as republicans: once they had got his brother out of the way, they would destroy the monarchy and himself. He refused to agree to exclusion, although his past record led many Whigs to believe that he would abandon James if sufficient pressure were put on him. Charles played for time, allowing Parliament to investigate the Plot but avoiding substantial concessions. Meanwhile, the panic created by the Plot subsided, the Tory backlash gathered strength, and his ministers ordered his finances so that, when he dissolved the Oxford Parliament of March 1681, he could be confident of surviving without Parliament.

At the Restoration Charles had been reluctant to throw his weight behind the old Cavaliers, but now he appealed unequivocally to his 'old friends', the Tories. They did not disappoint him. In the early 1680s the Crown and the Tories worked together to crush the Whigs and their supporters, the Dissenters. Leading Whigs lost their posts as JPs or in the militia. In many towns, the Tories sought to oust the more active Whigs from the corporation, often by procuring a new charter from the Crown. Usually, new charters gave the king power to remove members of the corporation at will. The commissions appointed under the Corporation Act had been temporary: after they had completed their work, Dissenters and other 'disaffected' persons had slipped back into office [**doc. 35**]. Under the new charters, the disaffected could be removed at any time.

Often chicanery and undue pressure were used to induce corporations to surrender their charters, but this did not worry the Tories if it produced the desired results – municipal power vested in 'loyal' men and the laws against political and religious dissent effectively enforced. Not all Whigs were excluded from office, in county or town, but those who remained were in a minority and were expected not to oppose the Tories' wishes (**62, 87, 97**). Before the new charters of the 1680s, there were many boroughs where Dissenters worshipped in defiance of the laws and Whigs accused of political offences escaped scot-free. The most important was London, whose inability to defend its charter against legal attack led other towns to surrender theirs without a struggle.

The polarisation of the political nation encouraged a politicisation of justice: "Tis now come to a civil war not with the sword but law, and if the king cannot make his judges speak for him he will be beaten out of the field' (**4**). The judiciary became solidly Tory; Tory sheriffs chose Tory jurors, and the full weight of the law was turned against Whigs and Dissenters, supplemented by extra-legal pressures, such as the denial of poor relief to those who did not attend Anglican services.

Charles II's regime of 1681–5 was perhaps the most authoritarian royal government of the century. It proved as well able as

Charles I's to crush its political enemies, even without prerogative courts. An incidental benefit of the new charters was that when James became king he was able to influence his first parliamentary election far more than Charles I could have done. The roots of this strength were not institutional but political. Unlike Charles I's Personal Rule, the Tory reaction of 1681–5 had the active support of a large section of the political nation: indeed, the government often had to restrain the Tories' enthusiasm. They assumed that the interests of Crown, Church and Tories were indivisible, a natural and logical assumption while Charles lived. Later, James's conduct forced them into a painful reappraisal of their position.

If Charles survived to live out his last years in peace, this owed as much to luck and the monarchy's inherent strength as to his own skills as king. For all his cleverness, perhaps over-cleverness, in diplomacy and intrigue, he seems never to have understood or trusted the men who made up the political nation or sat in Parliament. His distrust, frivolity and (despite his cynicism) openness to suggestion led him to embrace unwise and provocative policies. In the words of the Earl of Mulgrave: 'His great dexterity was in cozening himself, by gaining a little one way while it cost him ten times as much in another and by caressing those most who had deluded him the oftenest'. Despite the folly and irresponsbility he showed, Charles survived. This owed much to his sense of self-preservation and to the fact the 'he was not striving, nor ambitious, but easy, loved pleasures and seemed chiefly to desire quiet and security for his own time' (**27**). In that respect, Charles was well suited to the politically conservative age in which he lived. His brother, who tried to bring about major changes, lost his throne.

6   Religion and Ideas

After the legislation of the 1660s the Church of England was again the established Church, but was in some ways weaker than before. Those refusing to recognise any national church were now far more numerous. The sheer physical destruction of church buildings and furniture took years to make good and in some cases was never made good at all. The Church's organisation was restored much more quickly. Bishops, deans and chapters regained possession of their lands, new diocesan officials were appointed and visitations and other aspects of diocesan administration resumed.

The Church courts were re-established, but without High Commission* and Star Chamber* to back them up were only a shadow of their former selves. For a while they strove to resume their old functions, dealing with moral offences as well as wills, marriages and purely ecclesiastical business. On some matters, notably nonconformity, they proved less effective than the secular courts, as the punishments they imposed (such as excommunication) carried little weight. On others, they aroused the jealousy of the common lawyers and by the end of the century they were largely confined to cases in which there was no danger of their trespassing on the jurisdiction of the common law courts (**64, 120**).

The Church courts' diminished role symbolised the re-establishment of lay domination over the Church. Similarly, impropriated tithes*, confiscated from Royalists and restored to the clergy in the 1640s, were now returned to their lay owners. Convocation*, which even in 1640 had claimed to legislate for the Church independently of Parliament, effectively ceased to function after surrendering its right to tax the clergy in 1664. For both legislative and fiscal purposes, the clergy were now fully subject to Parliament.

If Laud's hopes of reviving the clergy's authority and autonomy were not fulfilled, he would have found other aspects of the Restoration Church more to his liking. Puritan* attempts to reform the Prayer Book services were decisively rejected. Most parish churches had altars, not communion tables, and parishioners received communion kneeling, rather than seated. Most, but not all, Anglican clergymen wore a surplice.

One should not, however, see these developments as evidence of a 'triumph of the Laudians' (**39**). They were well established features of the Church before Laud came on the scene and reflected a widespread attachment to the Prayer Book which continued throughout the century. Laud may have increased the Church's stress on ritual and ceremony, but in general his efforts had little lasting impact. The clergy's subordination to the laity increased, church interiors and the conduct of services still fell well short of Laud's idealistic standards, and the clergy still had to come to terms with the realities of village life (**100**).

A new High Church element emerged after 1660, whose adherents had by Anne's reign become the most vociferous, if not necessarily the most numerous, section of the clergy. How far these High Churchmen were 'Laudian' in inspiration is debatable. They expressed great respect for Laud and shared his concern for ceremony and for maintaining the Church's influence in society, but their outlook also represented a reaction to changes, inside and outside the Church, between the civil wars and the early eighteenth century.

In a political sense, the restoration of an effective, hierarchical Church was part of the conservative reaction to the civil wars. Many, disillusioned with evangelism and enthusiasm, came to see the merit of a Church which emphasised stability and a set form of service. Pepys's patron, Sandwich, once a Puritan, told him 'that things would not be well while there was so much preaching and that it would be better if nothing but homilies were to be read in churches' (**24**). Later, with the growth of Latitudinarianism and scepticism, the Church could be seen as the guardian of Christian values.

In short, the great appeal of the High Churchmen was that they stood for tradition and stability in a changing world. Yet although they were strong, they were not all-powerful. Many parish clergymen who had kept their benefices throughout the 1640s and 1650s stayed on after 1662. Many of these were moderate conformists, but some were more Puritan in outlook. Presbyterians* had, in 1662, to weigh their distaste for ceremonies and old-style prelacy against their commitment to a national church and their desire not to lose their livings or abandon their parishioners. There remained in the Church some like Ralph Josselin, who in more than twenty years' ministry under Charles II hardly ever wore a surplice. Others, like Baxter, refused to conform but did not see themselves as nonconformists and attended services conducted by the more Puritan clergy of the established Church. The Church remained broad, but with the balance of power swinging in favour of the High Church element.

The Church's most striking weakness was that large numbers of Dissenters rejected its spiritual and moral authority. Living in an age when religious pluralism is widely accepted, it is not easy to appreciate the arguments for religious uniformity which were so widely supported, especially by High Churchmen. Recent experience in much of Europe suggested that religious divisions within a state bred political confusion. Many also believed that only an effective church could maintain moral discipline and uphold Christian values, without which society would dissolve into crime, promiscuity and chaos: the conduct of the Ranters and early Quakers reinforced this belief. The attempt to restore a national church and to force Dissenters to conform to it was thus motivated by spiritual ideals as well as by social and political conservatism.

Whatever the motives behind the attempts to crush Dissent, however, they failed. Twenty years' unchecked growth had given the sects strength and self-confidence, while the state's apparatus of coercion proved unequal to the task, especially as some JPs sympathised with Dissent or disliked persecution. As fears of Popery grew, many Anglicans felt that Protestants should unite: a bill granting freedom of worship to Dissenters passed both Houses in 1680, but did not become law (**74**). When Dissenters were persecuted in the Tory reaction, the reasons were as much political as religious.

The fortunes of Dissent under Charles II were mixed. The incidence of persecution varied, some denominations being harassed far more than others (**76**). The greatest sufferers were the Quakers: many conventional Dissenters regarded them as Papists in disguise, or resented their seeking guidance from inward inspiration rather than from the Bible. The severity of persecution also varied over time: fierce, if patchy, in the 1660s; limited in the 1670s; very severe after 1680. The Indulgence of 1672, allowing for the opening of licensed meeting-houses, offered a breathing-space after the harassment of the 1660s, enabling the Dissenters to increase their numbers, so that they were better able to withstand the persecution of the 1680s. Finally, there were geographical variations. In general, Dissenters worshipped more freely in towns, where the corporation often failed to enforce the laws, than in rural areas, where the magistrates were gentlemen appointed by the crown. In many towns the laws were rarely enforced until the changes of magistrates in the 1680s [**doc. 35**].

The relative strength of Anglicanism and Dissent is hard to determine. In 1676, Henry Compton, Bishop of London, organised a religious census. Clergymen were to send in the numbers of Anglicans, Dissenters and Catholics in their parishes. While the figures for Catholics may have been quite accurate for much of the country (**90**), those for Dissent seem implausibly low [**doc. 36**]. The aim of the census was to enable Danby to prove to the king that the Anglicans were much the largest religious group, so the many occasional conformists ('church Papists' or Protestants like Baxter) were returned as Anglicans, as were the many whose religious convictions were lukewarm or minimal and who rarely, if ever, attended church. At the parish level it was not always easy to distinguish conformists from nonconformists, or to say to which sect the latter belonged [**docs. 36, 37**].

In a society where the majority of people were illiterate and received no formal education, it is not surprising that the religious understanding of many was limited or that some people's ideas were confused, especially after the recent ferment of debate. Some upland areas remained largely untouched by organised religion, despite the efforts, at different times, of Anglicans, Catholics, Baptists and Quakers [**doc. 38**]. In general, the Church was strongest in the larger, more compact villages and market towns of the South and Midlands. The main strength of Dissent lay in the larger towns, industrial communities and the more dispersed villages and hamlets of forest, pastoral and upland regions. Catholicism survived in pockets in the South and Midlands, bunched around gentry households, and in remote, hilly areas in the North and the Welsh Marches.

After making due allowance for the inadequacies of the Compton Census, it is clear that Dissenters made up only a minority, and not a very large minority, of the population. One reason for their limited numbers was persecution, but that was uneven in incidence and was often least severe where Dissent was strongest, in towns. Only a minority of English people lived in towns, however, and in rural areas the Anglican gentry, in their dual capacity as landlords and magistrates, could put pressure on people to conform. Dissenting and Catholic landlords did much to sustain the numbers of their denominations [**doc. 37**], but Dissent soon lost most of its gentry support after 1660 and the Catholic gentry were never very numerous.

It also seems likely that the appeal of Dissent was inherently limited. To belong to a 'gathered church' required a level of spiritual commitment which only a minority possessed: the initial excitement of conversion was often hard to sustain. One had to be tough and confident of one's righteousness to put up with the mutual criticism which many congregations practised. The emphasis of most Dissenters on the Bible as the source of authority would tend to deter the illiterate, although it did not always do so. As a religion of the Word, Dissent involved considerable intellectual effort: sermons could last for hours. For many, probably the great majority, the Church of England, with its set cycle of services and its participation in physical acts of worship, must have seemed intellectually less demanding and spiritually more edifying. It was not given to everyone to be spiritual athletes.

A final reason for the limited appeal of Dissent can be found, yet again, in the 1640s and 1650s. Laud's fall encouraged apocalyptic hopes of a more perfect spiritual order on earth, a rule of the saints. There were hopes that God Himself would bring this order into being, but if He did so, He worked in mysterious ways. Instead of His guiding the gathered churches towards harmony, they drifted apart amid acrimony. Confident predictions that the world was about to end proved incorrect, while the Ranters' excesses convinced many Puritans that they were heading not for perfection but for chaos.

The frustration of the hopes of the 1640s led to disillusionment. Many conservative Puritans turned to the Church as the only guarantee of order and stability. Most sects, instead of seeking to change the world, turned in on themselves and concentrated on maintaining their own spiritual purity. Even the Quakers lost their early exhibitionism and became quiet and respectable. The 'Puritan Revolution' shattered the broad consensus of the early 1640s and made a united Puritan front impossible: at the Restoration, most Presbyterians wanted comprehension, but other Dissenters sought only toleration. It also destroyed the Puritans' self-confidence, their belief that God was with them and that unlimited preaching and debate would produce a more godly and united society [**doc. 9**]. Finally, the excesses of 1640–60 provoked a reaction against 'enthusiasm' among Protestants of all kinds.

This reaction was seen most clearly within the Church, among the Latitudinarians. Whatever their disagreements, High Churchmen and Puritans like Baxter dealt in dogmatic certainties, although the former sought authority in the Fathers and the Church's traditions, as well as the Bible, while the latter relied on the Bible alone. This dogmatism led to bitter arguments about such symbolic points as the use of the sign of the cross in baptism. The Latitudinarians declared themselves weary of such wranglings. Surely, they argued, it was more rational and constructive to concentrate on the basic tenets of Christianity, on which all agreed, and on practical morality. Too much fervour clouded the understanding and distracted the clergy from their main task of encouraging people to lead better lives. Taken to extremes, this approach led some to reduce the essentials of Christianity almost to nothing, to develop an essentially functional view of morality (leading a good life was profitable) and to make religion so devoid of emotion as to be deadly dull. Under Charles II, however, the Latitudinarians injected a welcome coolness and common sense into the still ferocious debates about religion. They provided another element within the Church favourable to toleration for Dissent, while their lack of dogmatism made them more open than High Churchmen or Dissenters to the appeal of science.

It has often been argued that Protestantism, with its stress on the individual's interpretation of the Bible, was more conducive to scientific enquiry than Catholicism, which subordinated individual judgment to the authority or the Church (**117**). To some extent this is plausible, but many Protestants rejected scientific ideas which contradicted the teachings of the Bible and most Protestant churches imposed severe restrictions on intellectual freedom. In the second half of the seventeenth century, the most fruitful scientific activity took place in England and the Dutch Republic, where the established Protestant churches were comparatively weak. In England, scientific debate had flourished in the absence of ecclesiastical authority in the Interregnum and the momentum was not lost at the Restoration. Science became fashionable, in part because of Charles's patronage of the Royal Society.

For many, an interest in science went little further than idle curiosity. Evelyn described the Royal Society as 'an assembly of many honourable gentlemen who meet inoffensively together, under His Majesty's royal cognizance, and to entertain themselves ingenuously whilst their other domestic avocations or public business deprives them of being always in the company of learned men' (**75**). Much of the Royal Society's time was taken up with trivial matters and many 'scientists' amassed information with little idea of how to organise or analyse it. Alongside the dilettantes and eccentrics, however, were serious experimenters and statisticians, and popularisers who believed that scientific knowledge could serve a constructive social purpose: only by accumulating data could one begin to understand the world, and until one understood it one could not begin to improve it.

In terms of practical economic and social improvement, the achievements of Restoration science seem meagre. The Royal Society publicised new crop rotations developed in the Low Countries, but it is uncertain how widely farmers adopted them. It was easier to gather statistics on population or trade than to apply them to the practice of government (**45**). Perhaps the most important achievement of the new interest in science was to help to create a mood of optimism, often overstated, about the potential of human knowledge and the possibility of human improvement [**doc. 39**]. Science offered rational explanations for phenomena once understood in terms of evil spirits or divine wrath – or held out the hope that such explanations could be found. If the universe could be shown in some respects to function according to ascertainable mathematical laws, why not the physical world as well?

This rational approach to the world and the cosmos was potentially at odds with older explanations in terms of either the hand of God or occult forces. Some saw science as a threat to orthodox Christianity, or resented the cavalier way in which some of its proponents dismissed traditional authorities and explanations, but many found little difficulty in reconciling science and religion. Closer inspection of God's creation could increase respect for His achievement. To show that parts of creation obeyed mathematical laws did not necessarily cast doubt on His having established those laws, or on His ability to intervene arbitrarily if He chose. It took time for the belief to spread that God intervened rarely or never in earthly affairs, having created a wonderfully complex set of self-regulating mechanisms which required no further action on His part – and such a belief was never universally accepted.

Belief in occult forces did not disappear either, especially among the less educated, but became increasingly unfashionable among the educated elite. This helped to created a gulf between elite and popular culture which had not existed a century earlier. For example, in the later seventeenth century JPs and judges became reluctant to convict those accused of witchcraft, and the witchcraft laws were repealed in 1736 (**doc. 40**].

A growing emphasis on a scientific, rational approach served to undermine religious dogmatism and belief in the occult, but only within the educated minority, and even within that many were unaffected or only partly convinced. Some held beliefs which to modern eyes might seem incompatible. Sir Isaac Newton, whose discoveries did much to strengthen the concept of the universe as a self-regulating mechanism, denounced such a concept, was reluctant to deny the possibility of miracles, and dabbled in alchemy. Religious teachings were adapted to take account of new discoveries; occult beliefs continued alongside scientific ideas.

When all qualifications have been made, however, the new science and the reaction against enthusiasm helped to create, among the educated elite, a mentality, an intellectual approach, substantially different from that of the first half of the century. Religion became less a subject of dogmatic certainty, more a private matter, on which there was room for honest disagreement. The world was no longer seen as irredeemably corrupt, a snare and delusion through which one passed on the way to the perfection of the after-life. Many now saw the world as worthy of study in its own right — and why not, for it was God's handiwork. Growing understanding of the world led to a belief that man might one day be able to make his life happier, more comfortable and more secure. By improving crops and agricultural techniques, more food could be produced. By making better use of a nation's resources (not least its labour force) its wealth might be greatly increased.

Early Stuart writers claimed that England was overpopulated, its resources overstretched; providing for the poor seemed a huge and insoluble problem. By Charles II's reign, some expressed greater optimism. They no longer proclaimed that the end of the world was nigh, nor that mankind was irremediably weak and sinful, nor that life on earth was simply a painful preparation for the perfection and true happiness of the hereafter. They were coming to believe that the world could be improved – in short, in the possibility of progress (**112, 123**).

75

7 The Place of the Restoration in English History

It is often claimed that the 'English Revolution' permanently altered England, that it brought about (or completed) a seismic change in the structure of society and unleashed new ideas which, with the king's execution, irreversibly weakened the monarchy. Arguments that there were major social changes rest on the premise that the 'Revolution' was itself the product of a long-term process of socio-economic change, a premise which is at best not proven.

The pre-eminence of land in both the economy and society continued throughout the century. Agriculture remained much the largest employer, land remained the largest source of wealth, the quality of the harvest still affected the whole of the economy. In social terms, the continuing importance of the landed elite and of landed values was shown by the eagerness of those who made money in the law and civil service, in trade and finance, to buy country estates and establish themselves as members of the gentry. The structure of society was not to be drastically changed until the structure of the economy was transformed, over a century later, by the Industrial Revolution.

As far as other types of change are concerned, I have suggested that the new radical ideas of the mid-century found little support after 1660 and probably served only to strengthen the conservatism of the ruling elite. The Puritans' victory over Laud was a pyrrhic one: they emerged after 1660 divided, disillusioned and in many ways discredited.

The reaction against the changes of 1640–60 might seem odd, but only if one sees those changes as developing out of the interests and aspirations of the more influential groups in society. If, however, men were forced by circumstances into actions which went against their principles, if they were carried along by events outside their control, the reaction after 1660 becomes far more comprehensible. Most had not wanted civil war, the abolition of monarchy or religious confusion. They had no wish to be ruled by soldiers or to have the world turned upside down. The Restoration gave a welcome opportunity to return to normal.

Historians have looked hard for ways in which the events of 1640–60 could have weakened the monarchy, but have shown far less interest in ways in which they might have strengthened it. The most striking improvement was in taxation. The legislation of 1641 swept away the archaic, random assortment of feudal and property rights and regulatory powers which 'the Crown had accumulated over the centuries and which (as means of raising money) had often proved inefficient, contentious and unfair. This left Parliament only the customs at the start of the civil war – not enough to sustain its war effort – so in place of these old revenues it established the monthly assessment (a direct tax on land, with a fixed and predictable yield, ironically based on ship money) and the excise. Both were highly productive and although the excise was unpopular, Parliament could overcome the taxpayers' resistance because, like the French monarchy, it had an army at its disposal.

Thus Charles II inherited a fiscal system far more rational and efficient than his father's, as well as a population becoming accustomed to substantial, regular taxation. Charles's regime built on this foundation, notably by establishing permanent networks of collectors for the customs, excise and hearth tax by the 1680s. Sir George Downing also tried to systematise the Crown's borrowing, but his system collapsed in the Dutch War of 1672 (**104**).

This new fiscal system was not Charles's only valuable legacy from the Interregnum. If not all the governmental changes of that period survived the Restoration, one sees in the 1660s a greater administrative professionalism: a concept of service to the state was beginning to replace the older view of office as a piece of property, to be exploited for one's personal profit. Samuel Pepys never disdained an opportunity to make money, but saw the king's service as his first concern. His love of order and method was shared both by old Cromwellians like Downing and by younger men like Charles Davenant, at the treasury, and William Blathwayt, who became secretary at war. The restored monarchy also appreciated the potential benefits of the Navigation Act of 1651. Re-enacted and extended, it contributed substantially to the expansion of English trade and shipping, its enforcement greatly facilitated by another legacy of the Interregnum, a much enlarged navy.

Thus some of the state-building developments of 1640-60 helped to make the restored monarchy in some ways financially and administratively stronger than that of Charles I. This serves to reinforce a central argument of this book: that Charles II's regime was not a ramshackle structure, thrown together in a panic fear of anarchy in

1660. It was solidly based, potentially viable and intended to last. A political scientist might argue that the Restoration settlement did not solve the problem of where sovereignty lay (**119**). A constitution in which the supreme law-making power was shared between king, Lords and Commons could be seen as a recipe for confusion: what if they could not agree? To such an argument (if he understood it), a Restoration Englishman would probably have replied that it had always been like that, that the English had managed well enough in the past, so why change? The political scientist's view assumes that conflict between ruler and ruled is natural and likely, and that the latter would constantly be seeking to extend their power at the expense of the former, but these assumptions are rooted in modern attitudes, not those of the seventeenth century, in political terms a conservative age. When things went wrong, men blamed, not the constitution, but the men who operated it. Moreover, this tripartite legislature embodied that balance between the powers of the Crown and the rights of the subject which lay at the heart of the English constitution.

By trying to return to things as they should have been before 1640, the Convention and Cavalier Parliament sought to give permanence to the restored monarchy. If they failed, the reasons should be sought not in any inadequacy of the Restoration settlement, but in Charles II's and James II's failure to understand the practical limits on their conduct, imposed by the interests and prejudices of the political nation. James refused to recognise those limits, and paid the penalty. Charles made many mistakes, but was saved by his lack of ambition and a fundamental instinct for self-preservation.

Part Three: Documents

document 1
General Monk

Monk's chaplain describes how he carried his officers and soldiers with him.

The General had...his great council of all commission officers in the army. It was a pleasant sight to see the General at the end of a table, in a room full of officers, putting the question...and then an ensign to make a long speech to the contrary (who was but started from a corporal the other day)...but though he submitted to these forms, yet he kept an absolute authority by the prudence and artifice of those he trusted, but did it by the way of counsel and persuasion, and though he was good at driving, yet he was now forced to lead gently...The great care that was taken was to catechize the soldiers well, into the principles and first rudiments of their duty and obedience and to spirit them into an understanding and sense of the quarrel; for upon the meeting of the Scottish and English forces in the field, it was supposed...that they would with difficulty enough be brought to fight one against the other...

Gumble (**13**), pp. 140v–141r.

document 2
The Political Situation in December 1659

The Royalist Allan Broderick tells Hyde that the Royalists cannot exploit their numerical preponderance, and that all depends on Monk. Five days after he wrote, the Rump reassembled.

To my short-sighted view, the prospect appears thus: no interest in the nation equals that of monarchy, whether we regard the number, wealth, courage or birth of the persons sincerely devoted to it; but the numbers are generally ill-armed, unmodelled, uncounselled, the wealth hoarded up or spent in luxury; the courage entertained with private animosities, and birth extends little further than escutcheons and precedency, save in some few...The next is the Presbyterian, who would have half a king, half a commonwealth, their numbers declining with the absence of the former; all men growing up since 1646 being of the better sense, besides many worthy converts. The Independents, as they are in congregate churches...of Anabaptists, Quakers, Seekers, Singers, &c. are three parts women to one of men, whose noise is consequently greater, but effects disproportionate. The army mixed (though very unequally) of all these is united by a general maxim...of opposing the common enemy, nor do any private petulancies provoke them to forget the public danger, wherein they only exceed us and (almost deservedly) enslave us...

[As for Monk] his letter to the fleet and his protestations to Cargill (one of those sent to him by the committee of safety) positively assert the Rump. His other discourses and letters seem to aim at the Parliament of 1648. His conference of August last year gives me yet a better hope and what the honest man for his oath's sake concealed will, I hope, break forth with this happy opportunity; a sober man he is, ambitious of a good fame as much as great, though I doubt too much bigot in Presbytery...

Clarendon State Papers (**6**), vol. III, pp. 631–3.

document 3

A petition for a free Parliament

In January and February 1660 there were petitions, to Monk or the Rump, from at least nineteen counties, for a free Parliament. This is a summary of the Oxfordshire petition, presented to Monk and said to bear over 5,000 signatures.

1. That as they were freeborn people and subjects of England, that it was a privilege that knights and burgesses ought to be present in Parliament for the good of their country [i.e., county] and in many places in the countries are wholly left out, either by death or seclusion.
2. That all places vacant by death may be supplied, and that those that was secluded in 1648 may be a[d]mitted.
3. That no unusual, previous or foreru[nn]ing oath may be put upon any man that is to sit in Parliament, and that no taxes may be put upon us without our free consent in Parliament.
4. That the fundamental laws of the land, the privilege of Parliament, the liberty of the subject, the property of goods may be

asserted and defended according to the first declaration of Parliament when they undertook the war.

5. That the true Protestant religion may be professed and defended, a lawful succession of godly and able ministers continued [and] encouraged and the two universities...preserved and countenanced...

Rugg (**28**), pp. 40–1, corrected against British Library, Add MS 10116, fo. 60

document 4
The Rump's Declaration, 23 January 1660

Faced with calls for a free Parliament, the Rump issued this promise of elections, but insisted that only republicans should be eligible to sit. It also gave assurances on other matters.

I.   That the Parliament will provide forthwith to perfect those beginnings which are already made for settling the government...in the way of a commonwealth and free state, without a king, single person or House of Lords, in such manner that they may be governed from time to time by representatives in Parliament chosen by themselves, in whom alone the supreme authority of these nations doth and ought to reside, and by such as they shall appoint and constitute officers and ministers under them for the good of the people; and that the Parliament will make it their care to form the army and forces of these nations in such a manner that, whilst it shall be found necessary for them...to be kept up for the safety of the commonwealth, they may be wholly subject and obedient to the civil authority...

II.   That all proceedings touching the lives, liberties and estates of all the free people of this commonwealth shall be according to the laws of the land...

III.   And that they will make effectual provision for the countenancing of a learned and pious gospel ministry...And as to their maintenance, that by tithes shall be continued...as also that provision shall be made for due liberty of conscience in matters of religion, according to the world of God.

VI.   As to the present burdens which are upon the nation, the Parliament is very sensible thereof...and it is one of the greatest cares they have upon them how to give the people that ease which their condition calls for...which the Parliament hopes in some measure to do in a very short time...

Old Parliamentary History (**23**), vol. XXII, pp. 60–2.

Monk seeks to reassure the army

This is part of a circular in which Monk and his officers try to justify to the rest of the army their having readmitted the MPs excluded in 1648, as the best way to secure a new Parliament 'under such qualifications as may secure our cause.'

And to take away all just jealousies from you, we so assure you that we shall join with you in the maintenance of those ends expressed in the enclosed and do expect your cheerful concurrence with us. And we desire to take God to witness that we have no intentions or purposes to return to our old bondage; but since the providence of God hath made us free at the cost of so much blood, we hope we shall never be found so unfaithful to God and His people as to lose so glorious a cause. But we do resolve, with the assistance of God, to adhere to you in the continuing our dear-purchased liberties, both spiritual and civil. The reasons of our proceedings in this manner may seem strange; but if you duly consider the necessities of our affairs and the present state of things, you will certainly conclude nothing so safe to secure public interest and to engage the nations peaceably to submit to a free state...and it is the opinion of the truest friends to a free state that it cannot be consistent with the perpetual sitting of these members, being contrary to the nature of such a government...

Old Parliamentary History(**23**), vol. XXII, pp. 170–1.

The Declaration of Breda, 4 April 1660

This removed most of the more immediate anxieties which might lead individuals to oppose the king's return.

And to the end that the fear of punishment may not engage any, conscious to themselves of what is past, to a perseverance in guilt for the future, by opposing the quiet and happiness of their country, in the restoration of king, peers and people to their just, ancient and fundamental rights, we do...grant a free and general pardon...to all our subjects...who within forty days after the publishing hereof shall lay hold upon this our grace;...excepting only such persons as shall hereafter be excepted by Parliament...we desiring and ordaining that henceforth all notes of discord, separation and difference of parties be utterly abolished among all our subjects, whom we invite and conjure to a perfect union among themselves, under our protection, for the re-settlement of our just rights and theirs in a free Parliament, by which, upon the word of a king, we will be advised.

And because the passion and uncharitableness of the times have produced several opinions in religion, by which men are engaged in parties and animosities against each other (which, when they shall hereafter unite in a freedom of conversation, will be composed or better understood), we do declare a liberty to tender consciences, and that no man shall be disquieted or called in question for differences of opinion in matter of religion which do not disturb the peace of the kingdom; and that we shall be ready to consent to such an Act of Parliament as, upon mature deliberation, shall be offered to us, for the full granting that indulgence.

And because...many grants and purchases of estates have been made to and by many officers, soldiers and others, who are now possessed of the same, and who may be liable to actions at law upon several titles, we are likewise willing that all such differences...shall be determined in Parliament, which can best provide for the just satisfaction of all men who are concerned.

And we do further declare, that we will be ready to consent to any Act or Acts of Parliament to the purposes aforesaid and for the full satisfaction of all arrears due to the officers and soldiers of the army under the command of General Monk; and that they shall be received into our service upon as good pay and conditions as they now enjoy.

Gardiner (**11**), pp, 465–7.

document 7

'The General's Paper'

These proposals, designed to secure the Presbyterians' personal, political and religious interests, were put to Parliament early in May 1660 (see doc. 12). They show that Monk wished to impose strict conditions on the king.

1. The sales [of confiscated lands] to those now in service in the

army and navy...to be confirmed for ninety-nine years, at the reserved rents not exceeding a sixth of the full yearly value.

2. The sales of bishops', deans' and chapters' and crown lands to other persons, not of the army or navy, to be confirmed for sixty years, at a rent reserved of the fifth part of the yearly value.

3. The sales of lands of all other persons to continue in the purchasers' hands...till satisfaction be made with interest at six per cent and their charges, as in the case of mortgages. Excepted out of the act of confirmation: the purchases of all persons that sat...in the high court of justice for the trial of the late king or in the council of safety [also certain other exceptions].

4. The annulling of all things passed under any Great Seal since 22 May 1642, except the seal appointed or used by authority of Parliament.

5. That of the Acts and Ordinances passed by the late Parliament, the king confirm such as both Houses shall tender unto him; particularly to pass an Act taking away the court of wards upon the recompense of £100,000 *per annum*...

6. Excepted persons in the Act of Oblivion: [five of those actively involved in the king's trial].

7. The General to have the command of the army during life.

8. The exercise of the Protestant religion and ministry to continue in the same state as now they are, until an assembly of divines ...shall be called, so that thereby, with the Parliament, the government of the Church may be settled.

Lister (**17**), vol. III, pp. 500–1.

document 8
Reactions to the Restoration: Thomas Rugg

Rugg was a London barber whose 'Diurnal' is a mixture of extracts from newsbooks, gossip and his own thoughts.

Now the state of affairs began to appear barefaced, and the truly noble English spirit to be visible in the restoration of our most famous Charles II...who, having tired envy itself and overcome more difficulties than humanity could endure, was by a general vogue invited to the exercise of his kingly office, which, after a long interval of change and foolish endeavours of new governments, was to the dear cost of the whole nation found to be the most complete and perfect government that ever bore sway here, under which may we still live, but with that freedom that we have undergone slavery in the rest...

Rugg (**28**), p. 87.

document 9

Reactions to the Restoration: Edmund Ludlow

Ludlow, a religious and political radical, tries to come to terms with the fact that God has apparently abandoned 'the godly' by allowing the Restoration.

I am assured it was done by the wise disposing hand of God, without whose providence not a sparrow falls to the ground, much less the blood of any of His precious saints...; whose dispensations herein, as they have been righteous (in that the nation in general seemed not to be fitted for that glorious work which He seemed to be doing for them by the means of some of His poor people...) so I am confident that these very dispensations will...appear to be in mercy and peace to His poor people and to all who desire to live godly in the land, and that when in the furnace they are melted into one lump, they shall come forth as refined gold. But it's the Lord's pleasure they should take their turn in the wilderness... He seems to take the rod into His own hand to correct them for their disobedience and unsuitable returns to all those eminent appearances of His amongst them; Charles Stuart and his party not contributing the least to their restitution... Yet so it is that the Lord is pleased for the present to make them the tail, who before were the head...

Ludlow (**20**), pp. 149–50.

document 10

Dissatisfaction with the court

Of the many expressions of dissatisfaction with the court and with Charles's favour to the Presbyterians, this was perhaps the earliest, dated a week after his arrival in London.

'Tis not to be imagined how many are dissatisfied; innumerable flocks of people hovering here to see how they may light upon places and preferments: the court and royal party grudging at every favour to the Presbyterian, and they on the other side thinking they have not enough, and all that is done to them being wrought by the

General [Monk] has begot much murmuring at him; 'tis thought too much that Lord Manchester should be lord chamberlain and four or five others of the privy council, as Holles, Annesley, Mr William Pierpoint, Sir Anthony Ashley Cooper and Mr Secretary Morrice...and all this the General's doing...

Historial Manuscripts Commission, Fifth Report (**15**), p.184.

document 11
Attempts to limit the king's powers

In the weeks before Charles's return, the Presbyterians sought to restrict his powers and schemed to exclude Hyde from office.

By stories artificially related both to the General and his lady, your enemies have possessed them both with a very ill opinion of you...I look on Manchester as the prime author of this, who is set on from beyond sea [i.e., the queen mother]. I am the more confirmed in this since the message the Lords sent to the Commons to desire them to add Manchester to the others as commissioner of the seal...Though the legislative power may remain in the king, Lords and Commons, ...the executive was never questioned to be in the king; and though the name may be allowed him, how little that will signify when he parts with the militia I need not say...

Lord Mordaunt to Hyde, 4 May 1660, Lister (**17**), vol. III, p.100.

document 12
Attempts to limit the king's powers (continued)

This gives details of the legislation proposed by the Presbyterians and of the Royalists' attempts to thwart them: see also **doc. 7**.

A bill was twice read this morning, committed and returned to be engrossed whereby His Majesty makes this a legal Parliament, though the writ was unduly issued...Another for confirmation of all [land] sales till further order or satisfaction by Parliament to the purchasers &c was twice read and committed. A third for arrears of the army and navy is drawn. A fourth for tender consciences, allowing the exercise of religion as now it is, till all controversies be determined by a national synod. A fifth to take away the court of wards, with allowance to His Majesty of £100,000 per annum in lieu thereof... The last and main bill, for indemnity and free pardon, is in the hands of Serjeant Maynard, who will (if there be any time) report it tomorrow...

I daily confer with the best men before the House sits, and deliver out notes of directions, contrived by Mr Palmer and the ablest lawyers and perused by my Lord Southampton...and the soberest statesmen, by which all with whom I had any correspondence, and many new men, direct their votes. I speak seldom, taking to myself and giving.this maxim, that if any of our enemies or half friends move anything desired in my notes, that it be presently seconded and brought to the question, our number being much superior ...[Monk] did yesterday declare himself to Geoffrey Palmer as entirely the king's as any subject of his in the three kingdoms; but privately to him and this day publicly in the House he declared himself bound in honour and by his word to see all sales confirmed to the soldiers...

Broderick to Hyde, 4 May 1660 (misdated the 13th), *Clarendon State Papers*(**6**), vol. III, pp. 747–9.

document 13
The bill to confirm the fundamental laws

Be it enacted...that the Parliaments of England and the members thereof shall forever hereafter fully and freely enjoy all their ancient and just rights and privileges...and...that the Great Charter of the liberties of England...chapters 5th, 14th and 29th, with all acts heretofore made for the confirmation and observation thereof; the statute made in the time of King Edward I, commonly called *statutum de tallagio non concedendo*, with all other statutes since made against any tax, tallage, aid, loan or other charge not set by common consent in Parliament; the Petition of Right...with all the Acts therein recited...together with the several Acts made [in 1641, concerning Star Chamber, High Commission, Ship Money, forest laws and knighthood fines]...and all other statutes formerly made and unrepealed for the defence and preservation of the rights and privileges of Parliaments and their members, the lives, liberties, freeholds and properties of the subjects, against arbitrary and illegal taxes shall be and are hereby confirmed and shall be from henceforth forever inviolably observed...and that His Majesty himself and all his officers...and all his royal successors and their public officers ...shall take a personal oath duly to maintain, observe and execute all and every the said laws and statutes to the best of their power...

House of Lords Record Office, Parchment Collection, Box 12, Bill for the Confirmation of the Privileges of Parliament, 3 July 1660.

document 14

Debates on the Church, July 1660

These extracts from debates on a bill 'for the maintenance of the true reformed Protestant religion' show the positions of Anglicans and Presbyterians on doctrine and church government and the efforts of court spokesmen to shelve the matter.

Mr Throgmorton said he would not be for the Presbyterian government because he had taken the oaths of allegiance and supremacy and urged how Knox and Buchanan had written against kings if they governed not well, and said, no bishop, no king...

Moved by Sir Trevor Williams to establish the religion according to the Thirty-nine Articles and not only according to the Old and New Testaments [as the bill proposed] which all that own Christianity profess...

Mr Prynne said he reverenced the Thirty-nine Articles but thought it unnecessary to insert them in this bill...

Sir Heneage Finch said not one letter of the bill made good the title, saying the religion of our Church is not to seek, but we have enjoyed it long and therefore now should not be to enquire for it, but moved that it be referred to an assembly of divines, for which we ought to petition the king, and said there was no law to alter the government of the Church by bishops...[He spoke] again against the paragraph and particularly liberty to tender consciences, which he said no man knew what 'twas...

Mr Bunckley thought a moderate episcopacy might take in the good of both parties and urged the king's present inclinations and endeavours and said that episcopacy was more boundless than monarchy as it was used, saying some of them gloried to put down all lectures in the country and 'twas a fault to preach twice a Sunday, but said that government by episcopacy, if circumscribed, was to be wished...

Sir Anthony Cooper said our religion was too much intermixed with interest, neither was it ripe enough now to handle religion, but moved that the whole committee might be adjourned for three months and this debate laid aside...

The committee sate an hour in the dark before candles were suffered and those were blown out twice, but the third time they were preserved, though with great disorder and then 'twas voted, about ten at night, that the king be desired to convene a select number of divines to treat concerning this debate and the committee not to sit until October next the twenty-third.

Diary of Seymour Bowman MP, Bodleian Library, MS Dep. f. 9, fos. 54, 62–6, 77–85 (debates of 6, 9 and 16 July: the final extract, though under the 9th, seems to belong to the 16th).

document 15
The Worcester House Declaration

This contained the most extensive concessions offered to the Presbyterians

No bishop shall ordain, or exercise any part of jurisdiction which appertains to the censures of the Church, without the advice and assistance of the presbyters; and no...officials, as such, shall exercise any act of spiritual jurisdiction in these cases, viz. excommunication, absolution, or wherein any of the ministry are concerned, with reference to their pastoral charge...Nor shall the archdeacon exercise any jurisdiction without the advice and assistance of six ministers of his archdeaconry, whereof three to be nominated by the bishop and three by the election of the major part of the presbyters within the archdeaconry...We will take care that confirmation be rightly and solemnly performed, by the information and with the consent of the minister of the place; who shall admit none to the Lord's supper till they have made a credible profession of their faith and promised obedience to the will of God...and that all possible diligence be used for the instruction and reformation of scandalous offenders, whom the minister shall not suffer to partake of the Lord's table until they have openly declared themselves to have truly repented and amended their former naughty lives...

Though we do esteem the liturgy...contained in the Book of Common Prayer...to be the best we have seen...yet since we find some exceptions made against several things therein, we will appoint an equal number of learned divines of both persuasions to review the same and to make such alterations as shall be thought most necessary...and that it be left to the minister's choice to use one or other at his discretion...In the meantime, out of compassion and compliance towards those who would forbear the cross in baptism, we are content that no man shall be compelled to use the same...No man shall be compelled to bow at the name of Jesus...without reproaching those who, out of their devotion, continue that ancient ceremony of the Church. For the use of the surplice we are contented that all men be left to their liberty to do as they shall think fit, without suffering in the least degree for wearing or not wearing it...

E. Cardwell (ed.), *A History of Conferences...Connected with the Revision of the Book of Common Prayer*, Oxford U.P., 1840, pp. 292–6

document 16

The army, the militia and taxation

Here Andrew Marvell tells the mayor and corporation of Hull of events in Parliament, stressing that disbanding the army takes priority even over reducing taxation.

We have made a vote for bringing in an Act of a new assessment for six months of £70,000 *per mensem* to begin next January. The truth is the delay ere moneys can be got in eats up a great part of all that is levying...And that is all that can be said for excuse of ourselves to the country, to whom we had given our own hopes of no further assessment to be raised...it will be each man's ingenuity not to grudge an after-payment for that settlement and freedom from armies and navies which before he would have been glad to purchase with his whole fortune...there being so great a provision made for money I doubt not but ere we rise to see the whole army disbanded and, according to the Act, hope to see your town once more ungarrisoned...I cannot but remember, though then a child, those blessed days when the youth of your own town were trained for your militia, and did, methought, become their arms much better than any soldiers that I have seen there since...

Marvell (**21**), vol. II, pp. 1–2.

document 17

The accusations against Clarendon

Here an official at the French embassy sets out the claim, current in the queen's circle, that Clarendon had deliberately failed to enhance the king's powers, a claim based on a gross exaggeration of the monarchy's strength in 1660.

The chancellor believes the world is well governed when England is quiet;...he wishes [the king] to be a good Englishman and nothing more...He has always been against putting on foot the guards which the king has raised, no matter how evident the danger might be...This man does not understand the importance of that sort of power, especially for a king of England; also during these recent conspiracies he advised the king to disband General Monk's regiment, which was the last remaining of the army...He intended that the king should be guarded only by the affection and love of his subjects, who show four times a year that they do not know whether they love themselves...Everything he does shows the same weak and lowly spirit, natural in a lawyer...

When the king returned, he did so as master of everything. I beg you to ask the opinion of anyone well-informed – the queen understands this perfectly. He could have kept up an army of 6,000 men if he had wanted, everybody was at his feet, full of affection, being so weary of the severity of the last government...He could have established whatever religion he wished, he could have changed the form of government without opposition, he could have taken off the penal laws from the Catholics...Now, however, all this power has diminished, people have changed their minds, their ardour has been allowed to cool...since the king has done no great things, the ill-intentioned have regained courage...there remains a certain republican spirit among the generality of people...which now is regaining strength, since the government has lacked the strength and the boldness to master it in a manner as absolute, authoritative and acknowledged as that seen in France...Hyde wishes the law to govern, and so, to be accurate, he is more the minister of the law than of the prince...

Bartet to Mazarin, 31 January/10 February 1661, Public Record Office, PRO 31/3/109, fos. 49, 25–6 (the latter part of the despatch is wrongly entered under 14/24 January).

document 18

Disagreement about the Corporation bill

The Commons' bill to remove the 'disaffected' from corporationns was drastically amended by Lords. The Commons here claim that the amendments would destroy municipal autonomy.

The second amendment strikes out all the commissioners' names and the powers given to remove ill members and restore those who were unjustly removed, to which we cannot agree, because

1. The whole regulation of corporations doth consist of placing the government in right hands; which by the bill sent up was put in a probable way of being effected, by this amendment is not so much as thought of; provision is made for nominating mayors and recorders, but no care for other members.
2. Nothing enacted by their lordships seems to us to provide for present safety...
3. So total an alteration of the government may have an ill effect upon the free elections...
4. No care taken that, if [charters are] renewed, they shall have their old privileges, nor for putting in good men.
5. The reformation in the bill sent up, but temporary...These amendments would make a perpetual change; and we have no cause to believe it either so agreeable to the desires of the corporations for which we serve, or so consonant with our trust.
6. The intermeddling of justices of peace of the counties in corporate towns may occasion a clashing of jurisdictions and a disturbance of government...

Commons Journals (**10**), vol. VIII, p. 312.

document 19
Court faction and parliamentary turbulence

Daniel O'Neill describes the Commons' investigations into misgovernment in 1663 and blames them on court faction.

We are falling into the courses of the old Long Parliament with a much swifter pace than that did. Our purest Cavaliers are more troublesome and malicious inspectors into the king and his ministers' behaviour than ever Hampden or Pym were. Every day we have some mad bill brought in...The truth is, the disputes of the court have raised these spirits and their reconciliations cannot allay them; nor do I believe any other charm will, but that which I despair of, which is His Majesty's changing his present manner of living and strongly applying his thoughts to his business, which is governed little to the satisfaction of those that wish well to him or to the peace of the kingdom.

Bodleian Library, Carte MS 32, fo. 597.

document 20

Clarendon seeks to protect the Presbyterians

In February 1662 the Commons passed a bill which would have driven Presbyterians out of livings in the Church of England, even before the uniformity bill became law. Clarendon helped have the bill rejected by the Lords, despite threats from some MPs to withhold money.

At first all the bishops...were against it and most of the Protestant lords temporal. But my lord chancellor was resolved to oblige the Presbyterians...and at last got seven of the bishops to join with him...The Duke of York was likewise brought over by his father-in-law and the Earl of Bristol was vehement in the thing, and all the Popish lords. The Presbyterian ministers sent Calamy, Baxter and Bates that day to the chancellor to give him thanks. Some of the Commons going to the king the day before to desire him to express himself positively against the confirmation of the ministers, he said he had promised them at Breda the continuance of their livings; whereupon they said the Commons might possibly, many of them, be tempted not to pass the bill intended for the enlarging of his revenue if His Majesty would favour the confirmation of the Presbyterian ministers; to whom the king answered that if he had not wherewith to subsist two days, he would trust God Almighty's providence, rather than break his word.

Rawdon Papers(**26**), p. 138

document 21

An attempt to amend the uniformity bill

This proviso, introduced in the Lords on the king's recommendation, was rejected by the Commons.

Provided always that, notwithstanding anything in this Act, in regard of the gracious offers and promises made by His Majesty before his happy Restoration of liberty to tender consciences...as likewise the several services of those who contributed thereunto...Be it therefore enacted that it shall and may be lawful for the king's majesty...so far to dispense with any minister as upon 29 May 1660 was, and at present is, seised of any benefice...and of whose merit towards His Majesty and of whose peaceable and pious disposition His Majesty shall be sufficiently informed and satisfied, that no such ministers shall be deprived...for not wearing the surplice, or for not signing with the sign of the cross in baptism, so as he permit and bear the charge of some other licensed minister to perform that office towards such children whose parents shall desire the same, and so as such ministers shall not defame the liturgy, rites and ceremonies established in the Church of England...

Historical Manuscripts Commission, 7th Report, Appendix, pp. 162–3.

document 22
Clarendon's arguments for toleration

In March 1663 Clarendon drew up arguments in support of a limited toleration for Dissenters. Basically pragmatic and political, they were designed to appeal to a hostile Commons, but may also have reflected the king's views.

As to His Majesty's judgment of the most likely means to prevent public disturbance and to settle peace through his kingdom, as the king is far from thinking that a general toleration is the means thereof – he knows the principles of some men are inconsistent with all government and do naturally lead them to make disturbances – so neither doth he think that a universal denial of all indulgence will be the way to peace in this conjuncture, for that is as much too strait as the other is too large, and will give too great an opportunity to men of ill principles...to work on the fears and discontents of many others, who though otherwise satisfied in the government and re-solved to live peaceably under it, yet being cast into perplexity and troubles upon the account of their nonconformity, which their con-sciences inevitably oblige them to, will be drawn into such combina-tions as are usually the occasion of terrible disturbances...; whereas the indulging of those who have no community of interest or affec-tion with such men, will break and disappoint all purpose of that kind and prevent the union of many interests in a common opposi-tion against them who enjoy the benefit of those laws they suffer under.

British Library, Add. MS 4107, fo. 264.

document 23
Royalist political ideas

These extracts are from the addresses to the Cheshire quarter sessions by Sir Peter Leicester, in 1670 and 1676.

Now whosoever will more diligently examine the beginning of things
...will find that nations did not originally spring up into kingdoms
or commonwealths by the mutual consent of the people: for in the
beginning...all rule consisted in the heads of families, and in them
the first born by succession, without any suffrages or election, as it
were by a certain right of nature, was esteemed a prince of his whole
kindred, both in sacred and civil matters, who chastised offenders at
pleasure...and in process of time paternal authority grew up into the
name and power of kings...Now as monarchy is the most natural
form of government, so is it the most perfect and best form...far
above either aristocracy or democracy...

A good king or monarch that rules well (as, blessed be God, ours
doth) will always take care for the good of his subjects and will
observe the laws established and the rules of good government; and
if a bad monarch succeed, who would break the laws, he is only
punishable by God, to whom he must certainly one day render an
account of all his actions; but he is not to be resisted by his subjects
...He that goes about to limit his prince cannot be a loyal subject;
for that were to open a gap to rebellion; and if in one thing he may be
resisted, then certainly in another: and so such subjects will be both
judges and parties...I have shown before that...supreme power of
government in monarchs and kings cannot be derived from the
people: then it must needs follow that they have it from God: and
then it is in the monarchy *iure divino*...

Sir P. Leicester, *Charges to the Grand Jury at Quarter Sessions, 1660–77*,
ed. E.M. Halcrow, Chetham Society, 1953, pp. 57–8, 77–8.

document 24
The underlying strength of monarchy

*In about 1675 William III expressed a fear of a possible civil war in Engand;
Sir William Temple, English ambassador at the Hague, told him that this was
most unlikely.*

I told him that the crown of England stood upon surer foundations
than ever it had done in former times and the more for what had
passed in the last reign, and that I believed the people would be
found better subjects than perhaps the king himself believed them.
That it was, however, in his power to be as well with them as he
pleased, and to make as short turns to such an end; if not, yet with a
little good husbandry he might pass his reign in peace, though not

perhaps with so much ease at home or glory abroad as if he fell into the vein of his people.

Temple (**29**), pp. 153–4.

Burnet on Charles II

Gilbert Burnet included an assessment of Charles's character in his History of My Own Time, *published in the 1720s. This earlier version (c.1683) is perhaps more revealing.*

He is very affable not only in public but in private, only he talks too much and runs out too long and too far; he has a very ill opinion both of men and women, and so is infinitely distrustful; he thinks the world is governed wholly by interest, and indeed he has known so much of the baseness of mankind that no wonder if he has hard thoughts of them; but when he is satisfied that his interests are likewise become the interests of his ministers, then he delivers himself up to them in all their humours and revenges...He has often kept up differences amongst his ministers and has balanced his favours pretty equally amongst them...he naturally inclines to refining and loves an intrigue...He loves his ease so much that the great secret of all his ministers is to find out his temper exactly and to be easy to him. He has many odd opinions about religion and morality; he thinks an implicitness in religion is necessary for the safety of government and he looks upon all inquisitiveness into these things as mischievous to the state; he thinks all appetites are free and that God will never damn a man for allowing himself a little pleasure...I believe he is no atheist, but that rather he has formed an odd idea of the goodness of God in his mind; he thinks to be wicked, and to design mischief, is the only thing that God hates...

H.C. Foxcroft (ed.), *Supplement to Burnet's History of My Own Time*, Oxford, 1902, pp. 48–50.

Halifax on Charles II

As a senior minister in Charles's last years, Halifax here writes from first-hand experience.

He lived with his ministers as he did with his mistresses; he used them, but he was not in love with them. He showed his judgment in this, that he cannot properly be said ever to have had a favourite, though some might look so at a distance...he tied himself no more to them than they did to him, which implied a sufficient liberty on either side...

He had back stairs to convey informations to him, as well as for other uses; and though such informations are sometimes dangerous (especially to a prince that will not take the pains necessary to digest them) yet in the main that humour of hearing everybody against anybody kept those about him in more awe than they would have been without it. I do not believe that ever he trusted any man or any set of men so entirely as not to have some secrets in which they had no share; as this might make him less well served, so in some degree it might make him the less imposed upon.

Halifax (**14**), pp. 255–6.

Court faction

document 27

Ruvigny was better informed than most French ambassadors, as a Protestant with numerous contacts outside the court.

The council consists of ministers with a mortal hatred of one another, who seek only to be avenged upon each other at the expense of their master's service; this means that there is great uncertainty in the resolutions which are taken...[so] that one can never be sure of anything...

The courtiers are normally attached to Parliament and, following the movements of that great body, they often allow themselves to be drawn along, against the interest of their master, for they know by experience that the most sure way to gain advancement is to make a great deal of noise, which obliges them always to urge the king to satisfy Parliament, hoping that that assembly will give money, of which they are sure to have the largest share.

Ruvigny to Louis XIV, 6/16 April 1674 and 29 March/8 April 1675, Public Record Office, PRO 31/3/131 and 31/3/132.

document 28

The king regains the Commons' goodwill, 1670

Marvell describes, with disapproval, how Charles won over a majority of MPs by backing the Commons in a dispute with the Lords and agreeing to a new conventicle bill.

All that interval [a two-month recess] there was great and numerous caballing among the courtiers. The king also all the while examined at council the reports from the commissioners of accounts, where they were continually discountenanced and treated rather as offenders than judges. In this posture we met, and the king, being extremely necessitous for money,...told us the inconveniences which would fall on the nation by want of a supply should not lie at his door; that we must not revive any discord betwixt the Lords and us; that he himself had examined the accounts and found every penny to have been employed in the war...When we began to talk of the Lords the king sent for us alone and recommended a rasure of all proceedings. The same thing...that we proposed at first. We presently ordered it and went to tell him so...At coming down (a pretty ridiculous thing!) Sir Thomas Clifford carried Speaker and Mace and all members there into the king's cellar, to drink his health ...When the commissioners of accounts came before us, sometimes we heard them *pro forma*, but all falls to dirt...[The Lords] are making mighty alterations in the conventicle bill (which, as we sent it up, is the quintessence of arbitrary malice)...so the fate of the bill is uncertain, but must probably pass, being the price of money...

Marvell (**21**), vol. II, pp. 314–5.

document 29

The political watershed of 1672

Dering was one of many to see a major change in politics around 1672.

[After the Restoration] for twelve years more, we lived in peace, plenty and happiness above all nations of the world. But this blessing was too great to be continued long to those who deserved it so ill as we, and then the nation began to think the court inclined to favour Popery and France, grounding their suspicion upon
1.   The declaration coming out about this time for laying aside all the penal laws in matters of religion.

2. The second war made with the Dutch in conjunction with France, there being no sufficient visible cause to provoke us to it.
3. The departing from the Triple League...
4. The connivance at the Jesuits and priests, who did abundantly swarm in the kingdom and even about the court.
5. The conference between the king and his sister, Madame, the Duchess of Orleans, at Dover, the cause of meeting and the matter there debated and resolved on being kept very secret.
6. The employing of several known or suspected Papists in great places of trust, especially Lord Clifford, made High Treasurer.
7. Lastly to these, and much more than all these together, was the Duke of York's being first suspected and afterwards universally believed to be a Papist, which gave no unreasonable foundation to fear that, the king having no children, when the Duke should come to the crown the Protestant religion would be at least oppressed, if not extirpated.

Diaries and Papers of Sir Edward Dering, Second Baronet, ed. M.F. Bond, HMSO, 1976, pp. 125–6

document 30
Discontent with, and within, the army, 1673

The anxiety about France and Popery was increased by the raising of extra forces for the war.

They say the soldiers were ready to mutiny at their decamping at Blackheath only upon a report of their uniting with the French army; everyone takes the liberty to talk what the Parliament will do next session, nay some...say they wonder who durst print the articles of war, but that none dare put them in execution, and indeed they have not yet been proclaimed. They scruple the oath in it and say that to swear at large to obey the king's command is strange, for then he may command things [for] which the persons that do them shall afterwards be hanged...

W.D. Christie (ed.), *Letters Addressed from London to Sir Joseph Williamson*, 2 vols., Camden Society, 1874, vol. I, p. 116

document 31
Danby's thoughts on policy, December 1673

Danby here sets out reasons why the Commons must be given the policies they want.

State of the present condition of the crown, which cannot be amended but by force or by compliance.

If by compliance, then it must be by Parliament or infinite reducement of expense.

If by Parliament, by this or a new one.

If by this, they must be gratified by executing the laws both against Popery and nonconformity and withdrawing apparently from the French interest.

If by a new one, they will either desire comprehension or toleration of all religions but Popery, and as to France the inclinations will be the same, only the new one will in all likelihood press the crown to it with less respect.

And, as to money, it is probably to be feared that neither the one nor the other will give anything proportionable to the wants of the crown till satisfied in their fears as to France...

Browning (**40**), vol. II, p. 63.

Tory propaganda

document 32

The Exclusionist Whigs relied heavily on anti-Popery, accusing the Tories of being crypto-Papists. Here a leading Tory pamphleteer counters that accusation and alleges that the Whigs wish to start another civil war.

A legal and effectual provision against the danger of Romish practices and errors will never serve their turn, whose quarrel is barely to the name of Popery, without understanding the thing itself. And if there were not a Roman Catholic left in the three kingdoms, they would be never the better satisfied, for where they cannot find Popery they will make it, nay, and be troubled too that they could not find it. It is no new thing for a popular outcry in the matter of religion to have a state faction in the belly of it. The first late clamour was against downright Popery, and then came on Popishly affected (that sweeps all). The order of bishops and the discipline of the Church took their turns next; and the next blow was at the crown itself; when every man was made a Papist that would not play the knave and the fool, for company, with the common people.

R. L'Estrange, *History of the Plot* (1679), Preface.

document 33

A Tory moderate

Roger North, in his life of his brother, Lord Keeper Guilford, argues that to stress royal authority and the subject's obedience was not to claim that the king was above the law.

His lordship was commonly reputed a high flier or prerogative man. It was true enough that his judgment was to give the crown all its lawful prerogatives; and he would willingly have consented that it should have had, in some cases, title to more...But that he was not equally just to the people in all their rights, as well of form as of substance, is utterly false. If we justly regard his censurers it will be found that his chief blame...was only that he would not sacrifice the law to the iniquity of the times...while he was of the opinion that the Tory party, in the temper of those times, pursued the true interest of England, that is to support the Church and crown according to the legal establishment of both, he was a Tory as they called it. But when the Tory party, or rather some pretended leaders, exceeded in joining with such as exalted the power of the crown above the law and sought to pull down the Church; then he was dropped from the Tory list and turned Trimmer.

R. North, *Lives of the Norths*, ed. E. Jessopp, 3 vols., Bell, 1890, vol. I, p. 249.

document 34

Whig political argument

Much Whig propaganda was crude anti-Popery; this passage attempts a rational political argument, although the logic and history are both somewhat shaky.

The representative of the people, the Commons, whose business it is to present all grievances, as they are most likely to observe soonest the folly and treachery of those public servants...so this representation ought to have no little weight with the prince...The best of our princes have with thanks acknowledged the care and duty of their Parliaments in telling them of the corruption and folly of their favourites. Edward I, Henry II, Henry IV, Henry V and Queen Elizabeth never failed to do it, and no names are remembered with greater honour in English annals. Whilst the disorderly, the troublesome and the unfortunate reigns of Henry III, Edward II, Richard II and Henry VI ought to serve as landmarks to warn succeeding kings from preferring secret counsels to the wisdom of their Parliaments.

Behrens (**37**), p. 59.

document 35

The resilience of urban Dissent

This letter describes how Dissenters soon re-established themselves in Great Yarmouth corporation after the 1662 purge.

Between 1662 and 1666 [all but two of the bailiffs and justices] ever stood for the king and Church's interest in the late unhappy times, and in all the foregoing years the laws against Nonconformists were so effectually executed that not a conventicle was to be seen in the town but, if discovered, was immediately prosecuted. But in '66 when Mr Thaxter...and Capt. Huntington came to be bailiffs and Sir George England...a justice, the scale was turned, the Nonconformists then publicly met and not the least check on them...if you peruse the address to Richard Protector, you will find those chiefly concerned in it to have the greatest share in the government of this town from '65 to the present day, from whence the Nonconformists here took courage to contemn both the laws and the king's commands and to grow so numerous as they are.

Calendar of State Papers Domestic (**4**) *1676–7*, pp. 221–2.

document 36

The Compton Census, 1676

Designed to show that conformists heavily outnumbered Dissenters and Catholics, the census covered the province of Canterbury: the figures for that of York were assumed to be one-sixth those for Canterbury. The account of the province of Canterbury was by Archdeacon Samuel Parker.

	Conformists	Nonconformists	Papists
Province of Canterbury	2,123,362	93,151	11,878
Province of York	353,892	15,525	1,978
	2,477,254	108,676	13,856

AN ACCOUNT OF THE PROVINCE OF CANTERBURY

In taking these accounts we find these things observable:

1. That many left the Church upon the late [Declaration of] indulgence who before did frequent it.
2. Sending for the present enquiries has caused many to frequent the Church...
3. That the Presbyterians are divided. Some of them come sometimes to church; therefore such are not wholly Dissenters...
4. A considerable part of Dissenters are not of any sect whatsoever.
5. Of those who come to church, very many do not receive the sacrament...

Calendar of State Papers, Domestic, 1693, (**4**) pp. 448–50.

document 37

The nature of Nonconformity

These letters from the parsons of Adderbury and Over Worton were in answer to a questionnaire on Dissent in the diocese of Oxford in 1682. The second parish is more typical than the first.

Besides that indifferency and coldness in religion, and that worldly-mindedness which possesses the generality, we have a factious schismatical spirit which reigns amongst us; we have two fruitful nurseries unfortunately placed amongst us, one Quakers, the other Presbyterian.

As for the Quakers, I acknowledge my unsuccessfulness, notwithstanding my endeavours...for Bray Doyly, who is the ring-leader and lord of one part of the manor, upon any vacancy in it fills it with Quakers from other parts and, it seems, resolves to admit no tenants but such. They keep a constant meeting Sundays and Wednesdays in a house built upon his estate for that purpose.

The Presbyterians, about a little mile from the town, they keep a conventicle, peopled from all quarters round about...This has a very ill influence...especially upon this parish, for though we have very few indeed that wilfully and constantly absent themselves from the offices of the Church...yet they, many of them, will straggle one part of the day thither, when they duly attend the public worship of God on the other, and they seem to be like the borderers betwixt two kingdoms, one can't well tell what prince they are subject to. This...has been my great trouble, but unfortunately, living under a slack magistracy, has been out of my power to redress...

The Dissenters in my parish of Over Worton...are five women in four distinct families, persons of inferior rank, little sense and, I hope, no bad influence, they seeming weary of their ways and (as many others already) only ashamed to return. Two have been anciently Quakers, a third owns and pleads for that sect, but there is hopes of her return, the fourth was bred an Independent, but these follow no meetings and their only pretext is the viciousness of others. The other hath sometimes frequented the Anabaptist meetings, since the late times of Indulgence...Three of the Quakers' children I baptised upon my first coming thither, who continue of good report in our Church...

M. Clapinson (ed.), *Bishop Fell and Nonconformity: Visitation Documents from the Oxford Diocese, 1682–3*, Oxfordshire Record Society, 1980, pp. 1–2, 32.

document 38

Ignorance of religion

This anecdote is taken from the papers of Oliver Heywood, a Yorkshire Presbyterian minister, and shows how some remote areas remained largely untouched by organised religion.

On November 4 1681 as I travelled towards Wakefield, about Hardger Moor I met with a boy, who would needs be talking. I begun to ask him some questions about the principles of religion; he could not tell me how many gods there be, nor persons in the godhead, nor who made the world, nor anything about Jesus Christ, or heaven or hell, or eternity after this life, nor for what end he came into the world, nor what condition he was born in. I asked him whether he thought he was a sinner, he told me he hoped not, yet this was a witty boy and could talk of any worldly things skilfully enough...He is ten years of age, cannot read and scarce ever goes to church. His name is Thomas Brook, his parents died when he was a child.

Oliver Heywood, *Autobiography, Diaries, Anecdote and Event Books*, ed. J. Horsfall Turner, 4 vols., A.B. Bayes, Brighouse and T. Harrison, Bingley, 1882–5, vol. IV, p. 24.

Mathematics and Progress

John Arbuthnot stresses the potential contribution of statistics, or political arithmetic, to human progress, while admitting that they are not yet being used as they should be.

Arithmetic is not only the great instrument of private commerce, but by it are (or ought to be) kept the public accounts of a nation; I mean, those that regard the whole state of a commonwealth, as to the number, fructification of its people, increase of stock, improvement of lands and manufactures, balance of trade, public revenues, coinage, military power by sea and land, etc. Those that would judge or reason truly about the state of any nation must go that way to work, subject all the forementioned particulars to calculation. That is the true political knowledge...It is true [of some writers that] for want of good information their calculations sometimes proceed upon erroneous suppositions; but that is not the fault of the art. But what is it the government could not perform in this way, who have the command of all the public records?

Clark (**45**), p. 141

Decline of the belief in witches

In this letter from Exeter in 1682, Lord Chief Justice North, later Lord Guilford, described the judges' embarrassment at having to enforce the laws against witchcraft, even though they doubted its existence.

Here have been three old women condemned for witchcraft...I shall only tell you what I had from my brother [i.e. colleague] Raymond, before whom they were tried, that they were the most old, decrepit, despicable, miserable creatures that ever he saw. A painter would have chosen them out of the whole country for figures of that kind to have drawn by. The evidence against them was very full and fanciful, but their own confessions exceeded it. They appeared not only weary of their lives but to have a great deal of skill to convict themselves. Their descriptions of the sucking devils with saucer eyes were so natural that the jury could not choose but believe them. I find the country so fully possessed against them that, though some of the virtuosi may think these things the effects of confederacy, melancholy or delusion...yet we cannot reprieve them without appearing to deny the very being of witches which, as it is contrary to law, so I think it would be ill for His Majesty's service, for it may give the faction occasion to set afoot the old trade of witch-finding, that may cost many innocent persons their lives, which this justice will prevent.

Calendar of State Papers Domestic (4) *1682*, p. 347.

Glossary

Absolutism Authoritarian monarchy, like that of Louis XIV's France: see Daly (**49**) and Miller (**91**).

Advowson The right to nominate the clergyman of a parish, often owned by a layman.

Chapter The governing body of a cathedral, headed by a dean, which administered the cathedral's landed property.

Committee In both Houses of Parliament, bills were (and are) read twice by the full House and then referred to a committee, which goes over the wording in detail before returning the revised version to the full House for the third reading.

Conventicle An unauthorised nonconformist meeting.

Convocation The clergy's equivalent of Parliament. The Upper House consisted of the bishops, the Lower House of elected representatives of the parish clergy

'Court' This is used, in a parliamentary context, to mean the king's ministers and their supporters.

Deputy lieutenants Under the command of the lord lieutenant, these were responsible for organizing and, if need be, commanding a county's militia. They were drawn from the upper gentry.

Excise Whereas the customs involved duties on foreign trade, the excise fell on a wide range of goods produced and consumed at home, notably beer and other alcoholic drinks.

Hearth money A rough property tax: the more hearths one had in one's home, the richer one was likely to be. The poorest were exempt but it was still unpopular because the collectors, like those of the excise, could enter private houses in the course of their investigations.

High Commission The top ecclesiastical court which, in effect, exercised the jurisdiction which the Crown had taken away from the

107

pope at the Reformation. Always unpopular with Puritans, it was abolished in 1641.

Impositions Customs duties imposed without parliamentary consent. These provided a major part of the early Stuarts' revenue until they were abolished in 1641.

JPs (or Justices of the Peace). Chosen mostly from among the gentry, they were the key figures in county government, acting both as magistrates and administrators.

Militia A citizen force, commanded by the lord lieutenant and deputy lieutenants and responsible for local defence. As Parliament and the law did not recognise the existence of a standing army, debates about the control of the militia also involved the issue of the control of the army and navy, all being taken away from Charles I in 1642 and restored to his son in 1661.

Parliamentarian This can mean a member of Parliament, but in this book it is always used to mean someone who took Parliament's side in the civil wars.

Presbyterian Used in a political sense to describe the more moderate Parliamentarians, it was more properly a religious term, used of those who wanted a Puritan established church. Some Presbyterians were dogmatically opposed to bishops; many were prepared to accept them, provided their powers were limited. All disliked the ceremonies practised in the Church of England on one hand and the excesses of the sects on the other.

Puritan A much-used term which is difficult to define. It covers a wide spectrum of practice and opinion, but most Puritans shared a greater than average religious zeal and a preference for a church service without ceremonies and with the emphasis on preaching.

Star Chamber An offshoot of the privy council, this was in Tudor times popular with litigants, because it dealt with cases quickly, cheaply and equitably. Under Charles I it became unpopular as an instrument of political and religious repression and it was abolished in 1641.

Tithes In theory, parishioners gave a tenth of the produce of their land for the maintenance of the parish clergyman. In practice, the sums they paid often became fixed, and in many parishes at least some of the tithes were impropriated – i.e. paid to someone other than the clergyman; in many cases, to a layman.

Triennial Acts That of 1641 declared that Parliament should meet at least once every three years, for a minimum of fifty days, and laid down elaborate procedures to ensure that it would meet even if the king failed to summon it. The 1664 Triennial Act omitted both the minimum period of sitting and the machinery by which Parliament could assemble without the king.

Wardship Many landowners' estates were technically held from the king under archaic feudal tenures, by which an heir had to make a payment to the king on succeeding his father (livery), while the king became the heir's guardian if he succeeded while under age; usually, in fact, the king would sell the right of guardianship to the heir's relatives. These tenures thus imposed an occasional, but sometimes severe, financial burden on landed families. They were abolished in 1660, but the king was compensated with half the excise.

Bibliography

PRIMARY SOURCES

1 Baxter,R.,*Reliquiae Baxterianae*, ed. M. Sylvester, London, 1696
2 Browning, A. (ed.), *English Historical Documents, 1660–1714*, Eyre & Spottiswoode, 1953
3 Burnet, G., *History of My Own Time*, 6 vols., Oxford U.P., 1833
4 *Calendar of State Papers Domestic, Charles II*, 30 vols., HMSO, 1860–1938
5 Clarendon, Earl of (E. Hyde), *Calendar of Clarendon State Papers* ed. W.D. Macray and F.J. Routledge, 5 vols., Oxford U.P., 1872–1970
6 Clarendon, Earl of (E. Hyde), *Clarendon State Papers*, 3 vols., Oxford U.P., 1767–86
7 Clarendon, Earl of (E. Hyde), *History of the Rebellion*, ed. W.D. Macray, 6 vols., Oxford U.P., 1888
8 Clarendon, Earl of (E. Hyde), *The Life*, 3 vols., Oxford U.P., 1827
9 *Clarke Papers*, vol. IV, ed. C.H. Firth, Camden Society, 1901
10 *Commons Journals*, vols. VII–IX
11 Gardiner, S.R. (ed.), *Constitutional Documents of the Puritan Revolution, 1625–60*, 3rd edn., Oxford U.P., 1951
12 Grey, A., *Debates in the House of Commons, 1667–94*, 10 vols., London, 1769
13 Gumble, T., *Life of General Monk*, London, 1671
14 Halifax, Marquis of (G. Savile), *Complete Works*, ed. J.P. Kenyon, Penguin, 1969
15 *Historical Manuscripts Commission, Fifth Report, Appendix, Sutherland MSS*, HMSO, 1876
16 Kenyon, J.P., *The Stuart Constitution*, Cambridge U.P., 1966
17 Lister, T.H., *Life and Administration of Clarendon*, 3 vols., Longman, 1837–8 (vol. III consists of documents)
18 *Lords Journals*, vols. XI–XIII
19 Ludlow, E., *Memoirs*, ed. C.H. Firth, 2 vols, Oxford U.P., 1894

20 Ludlow, E., *A Voyce from the Watch Tower*, ed. B. Worden, Camden Society, 1978

21 Marvell, A., *Poems and Letters*, ed. H.M. Margoliouth, 3rd edn., 2 vols., Oxford U.P., 1971

22 *Nicholas Papers*, ed. G.F. Warner, 4 vols, Camden Society, 1886–1920

23 *'Old Parliamentary History'*: *The Parliamentary or Constitutional History of England from the Earliest Times to the Restoration*, 23 vols., London, 1751–61

24 Pepys, S., *Diary*, ed. R.C. Latham and W. Matthews, 11 vols., Bell, 1971–83

25 Price, J., 'The Mystery and Method of His Majesty's Happy Restoration' in F. Maseres (ed.), *Select Tracts Relating to the Civil Wars in England*, London 1815

26 *Rawdon Papers*, ed. E. Berwick, London, 1819

27 Reresby, Sir J., *Memoirs*, ed. A. Browning, Jackson, 1936

28 Rugg, T., *Diurnal*, ed. W.L. Sachse, Camden Society, 1961

29 Temple, Sir W., *Memoirs, 1672–9*, London, 1692

30 Thirsk, J. and Cooper, J.P. (eds.), *Seventeenth-Century Economic Documents*, Oxford U.P., 1972

31 Whitelocke, B., *Memorials of the English Affairs*, 4 vols., Oxford U.P., 1853

SECONDARY WORK

32 Abernathy, G.R., jnr., 'The English Presbyterians and the Stuart Restoration, 1648–63', *Transactions of the American Philosophical Society*, new series, vol. LV, 1965

33 Ashley, M., *Financial and Commercial Policy under the Cromwellian Protectorate*, Oxford U.P., 1934

34 Aylmer, G.E. (ed.), *The Interregnum: The Quest for Settlement*, Macmillan, 1972

35 Aylmer, G.E., *The State's Servants: The Civil Service of the English Republic*, Routledge and Kegan Paul, 1973

36 Barnard, T., *The English Republic, 1649–60*, Seminar Studies in History, Longman, 1982

37 Behrens, B., 'The Whig Theory of the Constitution in the Reign of Charles II', *Cambridge Historical Journal*, vol. VII, 1941

38 Bolam, C.G., Goring, J.J., Short, H.L. and Thomas, R., *The English Presbyterians*, Allen & Unwin, 1968

39 Bosher, R.S., *The Making of the Restoration Settlement: The Influence of the Laudians*, Dacre Press, 1951

40 Browning, A., *Thomas Osborne, Earl of Danby*, 3 vols., Jackson, 1951

41 Carte, T., *Life of James, Duke of Ormond*, 6 vols., Oxford U.P., 1851

42 Chandaman, C.D., *The English Public Revenue, 1660–88*, Oxford U.P., 1975

43 Childs, J., *The Army of Charles II*, Routledge and Kegan Paul, 1976

44 Christie, W.D., *The First Earl of Shaftesbury*, 2 vols., Macmillan, 1871

45 Clark, G.N., *Science and Social Welfare in the Age of Newton*, 2nd edn., Oxford U.P., 1949

46 Clark, P. and Slack, P., *English Towns in Transition, 1500–1700*, Oxford U.P., 1976

47 Coward, B., *The Stuart Age*, Longman, 1980

48 Cragg, G.R., *From Puritanism to the Age of Reason*, Cambridge U.P., 1950

49 Daly, J., 'The Idea of Absolute Monarchy in Seventeenth-Century England', *Historical Journal*, vol. XXI, 1978

50 Daly, J., *Sir Robert Filmer and English Political Thought*, Toronto U.P., 1979

51 Davies, G., *The Restoration of Charles II*, Oxford U.P., 1955

52 Davis, R., *A Commercial Revolution, 1660–1760*, Historical Association, 1967

53 Dowdell, E.G., *A Hundred Years of Quarter Sessions: The Government of Middlesex, 1660–1760*, Cambridge U.P., 1932

54 Everitt, A., *Change in the Provinces: The Seventeenth Century*, Leicester U.P., 1969

55 Everitt, A., *The Community of Kent and the Great Rebellion*, Leicester U.P., 1966

56 Feiling, K.G., *History of the Tory Party, 1640–1714*, Oxford U.P., 1924

57 Figgis, J.N., *The Divine Right of Kings*, Harper & Row, 1965

58 Fletcher, A., *A County Community in Peace and War: Sussex 1600–60*, Longman, 1975

59 Fletcher, A., *The Outbreak of the English Civil War*, Arnold, 1981

60 Forster, G., 'Government in Provincial England under the later Stuarts', *Transactions of the Royal Historical Society*, 5th series, vol. XXXIII, 1983

61 Furley, J.S., *Quarter Sessions Government in Hampshire in the Seventeenth Century*, Warren and Son, Winchester, n.d.

62 Glassey, L.K.J., *Politics and the Appointment of Justices of the Peace, 1675–1720*, Oxford U.P., 1979

63 Green, I.M., 'Career Prospects and Clerical Conformity in the Early Stuart Church', *Past and Present*, no. 90, 1981

64 Green, I.M., *The Re-establishment of the Church of England 1660–63*, Oxford, 1978

65 Habakkuk, H.J., 'The Land Settlement and the Restoration of Charles II', *Transactions of the Royal Historical Society*, 5th series, vol. XXVIII, 1978

66 Haley, K.H.D., *Charles II*, Historical Association, 1966

67 Haley, K.H.D., *The First Earl of Shaftesbury*, Oxford U.P., 1968

68 Havighurst, A.F., 'The Judiciary and Politics in the Reign of Charles II', *Law Quarterly Review*, vol. LXVI, 1950

69 Hazard, P., *The European Mind, 1680–1715*, Penguin, 1964

70 Helms, M.W., 'The Convention Parliament of 1660', unpublished Ph.D. thesis, Bryn Mawr College, 1963

71 Henning, B.D. (ed.), *The History of Parliament: The House of Commons, 1660–90*, 3 vols., Secker & Warburg, 1983

72 Hill, C., *Some Intellectual Consequences of the English Revolution*, Weidenfeld & Nicolson, 1980

73 Holmes, C., *Seventeenth-Century Lincolnshire*, History of Lincolnshire, vol. VII, 1980

74 Horwitz, H., 'Protestant Reconciliation in the Exclusion Crisis', *Journal of Ecclesiastical History*, vol. XV, 1964

75 Hunter, M., *Science and Society in Restoration England*, Cambridge U.P., 1981

76 Hurwich, J.J., 'Dissent and Catholicism in English Society: A Study of Warwickshire, 1660–1720', *Journal of British Studies*, vol. XVI, 1976

77 Jones, E.L. (ed.), *Agriculture and Economic Growth in England, 1650–1815*, Methuen, 1967

78 Jones, J.R., *Country and Court: England 1658–1714*, Arnold, 1978

79 Jones, J.R., *The First Whigs*, Oxford U.P. 1961

80 Jones, J.R., 'Political Groups and Tactics in the Convention of 1660', *Historical Journal*, vol. VI, 1963

81 Jones, J.R. (ed.), *The Restored Monarchy, 1660–88,* Macmillan, 1979

82 Kenyon, J.P. *The Popish Plot*, Heinemann, 1972

83 Kenyon, J.P., *Robert Spencer, Earl of Sunderland*, Longman, 1958

84 Lacey, D.R., *Dissent and Parliamentary Politics in England, 1661–89*, Rutgers U.P., 1969

85 Lamont, W.M., *Godly Rule*, Macmillan, 1969

86 Miller, J., 'Charles II and his Parliaments', *Transactions of the Royal Historical Society*, 5th series, vol. XXXII, 1982

87 Miller, J., 'The Crown and the Borough Charters in the Reign of Charles II', *English Historical Review*, vol. C, 1985

88 Miller, J., *The Glorious Revolution*, Seminar Studies in History, Longman, 1983

89 Miller, J., *James II: A Study in Kingship*, Wayland, 1978

90 Miller, J., *Popery and Politics in England, 1660–88*, Cambridge U.P., 1973

91 Miller, J., 'The Potential for "Absolutism" in Later Stuart England', *History*, vol. LXIX, 1984

92 Mingay, G.E., *The Gentry*, Longman, 1976

93 Morrill, J.S., *Cheshire, 1630–60*, Oxford U.P., 1974

94 Morrill, J.S. (ed.), *Reactions to the English Civil War*, Macmillan, 1982

95 Ogg, D., *England in the Reign of Charles II* 2nd edn., Oxford U.P., 1956

96 Outhwaite, R.B., 'Dearth and Government Intervention in English Grain Markets, 1590–1700', *Economic History Review*, 2nd series, vol. XXXIV, 1981

97 Pickavance, R.G., 'The English Boroughs and the King's Government: A Study of the Tory Reaction, 1681–5', unpublished D. Phil. thesis, Oxford, 1976

98 Plumb, J.H., *The Growth of Political Stability in England, 1675–1725*, Macmillan, 1967

99 Pocock, J.G.A., *The Ancient Constitution and the Feudal Law*, Cambridge U.P., 1957

100 Pruett, J.H., *The Parish Clergy under the Later Stuarts: The Leicestershire Experience*, Illinois U.P., 1978

101 Robbins, C., 'The Repeal of the Triennial Act in 1664', *Huntington Library Quarterly*, vol. XII, 1948–9

102 Roberts, C., *The Growth of Responsible Government in Stuart England*, Cambridge U.P., 1966

103 Roberts, C., 'The Impeachment of the Earl of Clarendon', *Cambridge Historical Journal*, vol. XIII, 1957

104 Roseveare, H., *The Treasury: The Foundations of Control*, Allen & Unwin, 1973

105 Russell, C. (ed.), *The Origins of the English Civil War*, Macmillan, 1973

106 Siebert, F.S., *Freedom of the Press in England, 1476–1776*, Illinois U.P., 1952

107 Skinner, Q.R.D., 'History and Ideology in the English Revolution', *Historical Journal*, vol. VIII, 1965

108 Sommerville, C.J., *Popular Religion in Restoration England*, Florida U.P., 1977

109 Styles, P., *Studies in Seventeenth-Century West Midlands History*, Roundwood Press, 1978

110 Sykes, N., *From Sheldon to Secker*, Cambridge U.P., 1959

111 Thirsk, J., 'The Restoration Land Settlement', *Journal of Modern History*, vol. XXVI, 1954

112 Thomas, K., *Religion and the Decline of Magic*, Penguin, 1973

113 Thomas, R., 'Comprehension and Indulgence', in G.F. Nuttall and O. Chadwick (eds.), *From Uniformity to Unity*, SPCK, 1962

114 Tomlinson, H., *Guns and Government: The Ordnance Office under the later Stuarts*, Royal Historical Society, 1979

115 Underdown, D., *Pride's Purge*, Oxford U.P., 1971

116 Underdown, D., *Somerset in the Civil War and Interregnum*, David and Charles, 1973

117 Webster, C. (ed.), *The Intellectual Revolution of the Seventeenth Century*, Routledge & Kegan Paul, 1974

118 Western, J.R., *The English Militia in the Eighteenth Century, 1660–1802*, Routledge & Kegan Paul, 1965

119 Weston, C.C. and Greenberg, J.F., *Subjects and Sovereigns: The Grand Controversy over Legal Sovereignty in Stuart England*, Cambridge U.P., 1981

120 Whiteman, A., 'The Re-establishment of the Church of England', *Transactions of the Royal Historical Society*, 5th series, vol. V, 1955

121 Whiteman, A., 'The Restoration of the Church of England', in G.F. Nuttall and O. Chadwick (eds.), *From Uniformity to Unity*, SPCK, 1962

122 Whiting, C.E., *Studies in English Puritanism 1660–88*, Cass, 1968

123 Wilson, C., *England's Apprenticeship, 1603–1763*, Longman, 1965

124 Wilson, C. *Profit and Power: A Study of England and the Dutch Wars*, Longman, 1957

125 Witcombe, D.T., *Charles II and the Cavalier House of Commons, 1663–74*, Manchester U.P., 1966

126 Wrightson, K., *English Society, 1580–1680*, Hutchinson, 1982

127 Wrightson, K. and Levine, D., *Poverty and Piety in an English Village: Terling, 1525–1700*, Academic Press, 1979

Index

Index